# THE EMERGENCE
# OF BUDDHISM

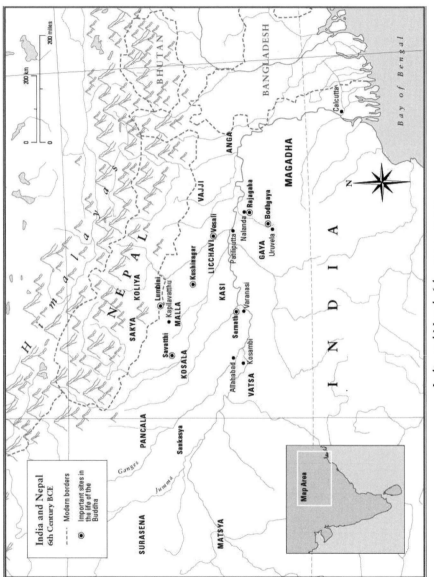

India and Nepal, 6th century B.C.E.

# THE EMERGENCE OF BUDDHISM

Jacob N. Kinnard

Greenwood Guides to Historic Events of the Ancient World
*Bella Vivante, Series Editor*

GREENWOOD PRESS
Westport, Connecticut • London

**Library of Congress Cataloging-in-Publication Data**

Kinnard, Jacob N.
  The emergence of Buddhism / Jacob N. Kinnard.
      p. cm. — (Greenwood guides to historic events of the ancient world)
    Includes bibliographical references and index.
    ISBN 0–313–32838–2 (alk. paper)
    1. Buddhism—India—History.  I. Title.  II. Series.
BQ286.K53   2006
294.30934—dc22        2006009758

British Library Cataloguing in Publication Data is available.

Library of Congress Catalog Card Number: 2006009758
ISBN: 0–313–32838–2

First published in 2006

Greenwood Press, 88 Post Road West, Westport, CT 06881
An imprint of Greenwood Publishing Group, Inc.
www.greenwood.com

Printed in the United States of America

The paper used in this book complies with the
Permanent Paper Standard issued by the National
Information Standards Organization (Z39.48–1984).

10  9  8  7  6  5  4  3  2  1

# CONTENTS

Series Foreword *by Bella Vivante*                                              vii

Preface                                                                        xiii

Chronology of Significant Events in the Emergence of Buddhism                    xv

Historical Overview: The Context Out of Which
Buddhism Emerged                                                               xix

**Chapter 1.**   The Life of the Buddha                                          1

**Chapter 2.**   The Establishment of Buddhism in India                         15

**Chapter 3.**   The Expansion of Buddhism in India                             29

**Chapter 4.**   The Continued Presence of the Buddha                           43

**Chapter 5.**   The Emergence of the Mahayana                                  57

**Chapter 6.**   Conclusion: The Decline of Buddhism in India
                 and Its Rise Elsewhere                                         69

Biographical Sketches                                                           79

Primary Documents                                                               95

Glossary of Selected Terms                                                     145

Annotated Bibliography                                                         149

Index                                                                          161

*Photo essay follows Chapter 6*

# SERIES FOREWORD

As a professor and scholar of the ancient Greek world, I am often asked by students and scholars of other disciplines, why study antiquity? What possible relevance could human events from two, three, or more thousand years ago have to our lives today? This questioning of the continued validity of our historical past may be the offshoot of the forces shaping the history of the American people. Proud of forging a new nation out of immigrants wrenched willingly or not from their home soils, Americans have experienced a liberating headiness of separation from traditional historical demands on their social and cultural identity. The result has been skepticism about the very validity of that historical past. Some of that skepticism is healthy and serves constructive purposes of scholarly inquiry. Questions of how, by whom, and in whose interest "history" is written are valid questions pursued by contemporary historians striving to uncover the multiple forces shaping any historical event and the multilayered social consequences that result. But the current academic focus on "presentism"—the concern with only recent events and a deliberate ignoring of premodern eras—betrays an extreme distortion of legitimate intellectual inquiry. This stress on the present seems to have deepened in the early years of the twenty-first century. The cybertechnological explosions of the preceding decades seem to have propelled us into a new cultural age requiring new rules that make the past appear all the more obsolete.

So again I ask, why study ancient cultures? In the past year, the United States' occupation of Iraq, after it ousted that nation's heinous regime, has kept Iraq in the forefront of the news. The land base of Iraq is ancient Mesopotamia, "the land between the rivers" of the Tigris and the

Euphrates, two of the four rivers in the biblical Garden of Eden (Genesis 2). Called "the cradle of civilization," this area witnessed the early development of a centrally organized, hierarchical social system that utilized the new technology of writing to administer an increasingly complex state.

Is there a connection between the ancient events, literature, and art coming out of this land and the contemporary events? Michael Wood, in his educational video *Iraq: The Cradle of Civilization*, produced shortly after the 1991 Gulf War, makes this connection explicit—between the people, their way of interacting with their environment, and even the cosmological stories they create to explain and define their world.

Study of the ancient world, like study of contemporary cultures other than one's own, has more than academic or exotic value. First, study of the past seeks meaning beyond solely acquiring factual knowledge. It strives to understand the human and social dynamics that underlie any historical event and what these underlying dynamics teach us about ourselves as human beings in interaction with one another. Study of the past also encourages deeper inquiry than what appears to some as the "quaint" observation that this region of current and recent conflict could have served as a biblical ideal or as a critical marker in the development of world civilizations. In fact, these apparently quaint dimensions can serve as the hook that piques our interest into examining the past and discovering what it may have to say to us today. Not an end in itself, this knowledge forms the bedrock for exploring deeper meanings.

Consider, for example, the following questions: What does it mean that three major world religions—Judaism, Christianity, and Islam—developed out of the ancient Mesopotamian worldview? (In this view, the world, and hence its gods, were seen as being in perpetual conflict with one another and with the environment, and death was perceived as a matter of despair and desolation.) What does it mean that Western forms of thinking derived from the particular intellectual revolution of archaic Greece that developed into what is called "rational discourse," ultimately systematized by Aristotle in the fourth century B.C.E.? How does this thinking, now fundamental to Western discourse, shape how we see the world and ourselves, and how we interact with one another? And how does it affect our ability, or lack thereof, to communicate intelligibly with people with differently framed cultural perceptions? What, ultimately, do we gain from being aware of the origin and development of these fundamental features of our thinking and beliefs?

In short, knowing the past is essential for knowing ourselves in the present. Without an understanding of where we came from, and the journey we took to get where we are today, we cannot understand why we think or act the way we do. Nor, without an understanding of historical development, are we in a position to make the kinds of constructive changes necessary to advance as a society. Awareness of the past gives us the resources necessary to make comparisons between our contemporary world and past times. It is from these comparisons that we can assess both the advances we have made as human societies and those aspects that can still benefit from change. Hence, knowledge of the past is crucial for shaping our individual and social identities, providing us with the resources to make intelligent, aware, and informed decisions for the future.

All ancient societies, whether significant for the evolution of Western ideas and values, or developed largely separate from the cultures that more directly influenced Western civilization, such as China, have important lessons to teach us. For fundamentally they all address questions that have faced every human individual and every human society that has ever existed. Because ancient civilizations erected great monuments of themselves in stone, writings, and the visual arts—all enduring material evidence—we can view how these ancient cultures dealt with many of the same questions we face today. And we learn the consequences of the actions taken by people in other societies and times that, ideally, should help us as we seek solutions to contemporary issues. Thus it was that President John F. Kennedy wrote of his reliance upon Thucydides' treatment of the devastating war between the ancient Greek city-states of Athens and Sparta (see the volume on the Peloponnesian War) in his study of exemplary figures, *Profiles in Courage*.

This series seeks to fulfill this goal both collectively and in the individual volumes. The individual volumes examine key events, trends, and developments in world history in ancient times that are central to the secondary school and lower-level undergraduate history curriculum and that form standard topics for student research. From a vast field of potential subjects, these selected topics emerged after consultations with scholars, educators, and librarians. Each book in the series can be described as a "library in a book." Each one presents a chronological timeline and an initial factual overview of its subject, three to five topical essays that examine the subject from diverse perspectives and for its various consequences, a concluding essay providing current perspectives on the event, biographies of key players, a selection of primary documents, illustrations, a glossary, and an index. The concept of the series is to provide ready-reference materials that include a quick, in-depth examination of the topic and insightful guidelines for interpretive analysis, suitable for student research and designed to stimulate critical thinking. The authors are all scholars of the topic in their respective fields, selected both on the basis of their expertise and for their ability to bring their scholarly knowledge to a wider audience in an engaging and clear way. In these regards, this series follows the concept and format of the Greenwood Guides to Historic Events of the Twentieth Century, the Fifteenth to Nineteenth Centuries, and the Medieval World.

All the works in this series deal with historical developments in early ancient civilizations, almost invariably postdating the emergence of writing and of hierarchical dynastic social structures. Perhaps only incidentally do they deal with what historians call the Paleolithic Age (Old Stone Age), the period from about 25,000 B.C.E. onward, characterized by nomadic, hunting-gathering societies; or the Neolithic Age (New Stone Age), the period of the earliest development of agriculture and, hence, settled societies, one of the earliest dating to about 7000 B.C.E. at Çatal Höyük in south-central Turkey.

The earliest dates covered by the books in this series are the fourth to second millennia B.C.E., for the building of the pyramids in Egypt, the examination of the Trojan War, and the Bronze Age civilizations of the eastern Mediterranean. Most volumes deal with events in the first millennium B.C.E. to the early centuries of the first millennium C.E. Some treat the development of civilizations, such as the volume on the rise of the Han Empire in China, or the separate volumes on the rise and on the decline and fall of the Roman Empire. Some highlight major personalities and their empires, such as the volumes on Cleopatra VII of Ptolemaic Egypt, and on Justinian and the beginnings of the Byzantine Empire in eastern Greece and Constantinople (Istanbul). Three volumes examine the emergence in antiquity of religious movements that form major contemporary world systems of belief—Judaism, Buddhism, and Christianity. (Islam is being treated in the parallel Medieval World series.) And two volumes focus on technological developments, one on the building of the pyramids and one on other ancient technologies.

Each book examines the complexities of the forces shaping the development of its subject and the historical consequences. Thus, for example, the volume on the fifth-century-B.C.E. Greek Peloponnesian War explores the historical causes of the war, the nature of the combatants' actions, and how these reflect the thinking of the period. A particular issue, which may seem strange to some and timely to others, is how a city like Athens, with its proto-democratic political organization and its outstanding achievements in architecture, sculpture, painting, drama, and philosophy, could engage in openly imperialist policies of land conquest and of vicious revenge against anyone who countered them. Rather than trying to gloss over the contradictions that emerge, these books conscientiously explore whatever tensions arise in the ancient material, both to portray more completely the ancient event and to highlight the fact that no historical occurrence is simply determined. Sometimes societies that we admire in some ways (such as ancient Athens for their artistic achievements and democratic political experiments) may prove deeply troublesome in other ways (such as what we see as their reprehensible conduct in war and brutal subjection of other Greek communities). Consequently, the reader is empowered to make informed, well-rounded judgments on the events and actions of the major players.

We offer this series as an invitation to explore the past in various ways. We anticipate that from its volumes the reader will gain a better appreciation of the historical events and forces that shaped the lives of our ancient forebears and that continue to shape our thinking, values, and actions today. However remote in time and culture these ancient civilizations may at times appear, ultimately they show us that the questions confronting human beings of any age are timeless and that the examples of the past can provide valuable insights into our understanding of the present and the future.

Bella Vivante
University of Arizona

# PREFACE

Buddhism began humbly in a small village in what is now the southern plains of Nepal, when Siddhartha Gautama, the son of a local ruler, a prince destined to be king, made the decision to leave his home and family and his royal future, and set out in search of spiritual enlightenment. This was not, however, a selfish abandonment of responsibility. Rather, he had seen and felt the sufferings of human beings in the world, and was deeply affected by this fundamental aspect of human existence, to the point that he was compelled to set out on a quest to alleviate this suffering, with no other motive than an intense compassion for his fellow human beings. After several years of intense spiritual striving, he discovered a clear and straightforward path to attain salvation, a means to escape the sufferings of the world, and he made the decision to share his discovery by teaching. The religion that Siddhartha Gautama founded, Buddhism, has in the course of its 2,500-year history spread to nearly every region of the world. To do so, it has had to adapt to a vast array of different cultural, linguistic, and geographical settings.

As it has spread, it has by necessity also changed, expanding to adapt to its myriad settings, incorporating local beliefs and practices, and shifting to accommodate the often-fluid social and political contexts. The Buddhist tradition embodies an incredible variety of beliefs and practices. There is no central Buddhist organization, no single authoritative text, no simple set of defining practices. Buddhism is, to its core, a pluralistic religion. It has absorbed local traditions, responded to historical events, and philosophically evolved and re-evolved. In many ways, it has been a religious tradition in perpetual flux.

Despite its incredible diversity, though, and its ever-changing character, there are also elements that cut across the many contexts in which Buddhism and Buddhists flourish—beliefs and practices that, although perhaps slightly different depending on their specific settings, could be recognized and practiced by all Buddhists. For instance, Buddhists throughout the world recite the ancient formula known as the Three Refuges: "I go for refuge in the Buddha, I go for refuge in the *Dharma*, I go for refuge in the *Sangha*." Furthermore, certain core philosophical tenets and beliefs that are said to have been articulated by the Buddha himself over 2,500 years ago still serve as the spiritual and ethical core for Buddhists throughout the world—the impermanence of all things, *karma*, *nirvana*, and renunciation. Thus, as much as we must pay attention to the diverse contexts and beliefs and practices, we can also fruitfully examine the Buddhist tradition as a whole.

Perhaps the single most significant unifying factor for the world's diverse Buddhist populations is the figure of the Buddha himself. Although the various schools of Buddhism have very different specific understandings of and attitudes toward the Buddha, each of them, without exception, recognizes, respects, and reveres him. What makes the Buddha so significant in Buddhism is not simply the fact that he is the founder of the religion, though. The Buddha serves as the template for every Buddhist, the model for the life of the individual. It is not enough simply to receive and understand his teachings, or to worship him. Rather, one must strive to be like the Buddha—to replicate his life, essentially.

In the pages that follow, we will explore the origins of this rich and complex religious tradition, examining the social and philosophical context out of which the Buddha and Buddhism emerged. We will delve into the person and personality of the Buddha and examine the central doctrines of the religion that he founded; we will explore the religious community that formed around this founder and his teachings, and see that his followers were able to spread their teacher's message after his death.

# CHRONOLOGY OF SIGNIFICANT EVENTS IN THE EMERGENCE OF BUDDHISM

| | |
|---|---|
| **16th century** B.C.E. | Development of Vedic religious worldview and ritual practice<br>Emergence of important Hindu philosophical schools of Mimamsa, Samkhya, and Vedanta |
| **800–500** B.C.E. | Composition of *Upanishads* |
| **552–479** B.C.E. | Life of Confucius |
| **c. 500** B.C.E. | Life of Lao-tzu |
| **c. 480** B.C.E. | Birth of the Buddha in Kapilavastu |
| **c. 450** B.C.E. | The Buddha's enlightenment and first sermon |
| **c. 405** B.C.E. | Death of the Buddha |
| **c. 405** B.C.E. | First Buddhist council, at Rajagriha |
| **c. 350** B.C.E. | Second Buddhist council, at Vaishali |
| **327–325** B.C.E. | Alexander the Great in India |
| **272** B.C.E. | Ashoka ascends the throne in India |
| **c. 250** B.C.E. | Third Buddhist council, at Pataliputra |
| **247** B.C.E. | Mahinda introduces Buddhism to Sri Lanka |
| **231** B.C.E. | Death of Ashoka |

| | |
|---|---|
| **200 B.C.E.** | Stupa construction at Sanchi begins |
| **2nd century B.C.E.** | Emergence of Mahayana Buddhism<br>*Perfection of Wisdom* (*Prajnaparamita*) literature composed |
| **1st century B.C.E.** | Theravada Buddhist Canon (*Tipitaka*) completed in Sri Lanka, committed to writing<br>*Questions of King Milinda* (*Milinda-panha*) composed |
| **68 B.C.E.** | Buddhist missionaries arrive in China at the court of Emperor Ming |
| **c. 100 C.E.** | Fourth Buddhist council, held either at Jalandhar or in Kashmir (sources conflict)<br>Indian Buddhists settle in Southeast Asia |
| **c. 150–250 C.E.** | Life of Nagarjuna |
| **4th century C.E.** | Rise of Vajrayana Buddhism |
| **320–467 C.E.** | Nalanda University constructed |
| **350–650 C.E.** | Gupta dynasty in India, flourishing of Buddhist art in India |
| **372 C.E.** | Chinese monks bring Buddhism to Korea |
| **399–414 C.E.** | Faxian travels to India |
| **420 C.E.** | Schools of Tiantai, Huayan, Chan, and Jingtu appear in China |
| **6th century C.E.** | Burma adopts Theravada Buddhism |
| **c. 525 C.E.** | Bodhidharma arrives in China |
| **526 C.E.** | Vinaya school founded in Korea |
| **527 C.E.** | Korea accepts Buddhism |
| **552 C.E.** | Buddhism enters Japan from Korea |
| **589 C.E.** | First Chinese Buddhist commentaries written |
| **594 C.E.** | Buddhism becomes the official religion of Japan |

| | |
|---|---|
| **7th century** C.E. | Mahayana Buddhism adopted in Indonesia |
| **c. 600** C.E. | First diffusion of Buddhism in Tibet |
| **618–650** C.E. | Life of Songtsen Gampo; establishment of Buddhism in Tibet |
| **618–907** C.E. | Chinese T'ang dynasty; golden age of Buddhism in China |

# HISTORICAL OVERVIEW: THE CONTEXT OUT OF WHICH BUDDHISM EMERGED

## THE BRAHMANICAL WORLD

The founder of Buddhism, Siddhartha Gautama, was by birth what we would now call "a Hindu," and although Siddhartha was highly critical of the religion into which he was born, and although the movement that he founded broke with this dominant religious tradition in significant ways, it also did not emerge from a religious vacuum. Indeed, it is important to recognize that Buddhism was at the start very much a reform movement from within Hinduism. It is thus essential to understand something of the religious worldview of sixth-century-B.C.E. India in order to understand the Buddha's own religious worldview and why Buddhism took the particular shape that it did. We must, in a sense, acquaint ourselves with the basic religious and philosophical vocabulary of the time.

The dominant religion in the northern Indian world into which the Buddha was born was Brahmanism—the word "Hinduism" is a foreign label describing the diverse religious culture of India, first used by Arab traders in the eighteenth century—a religion based on a body of texts called the *Vedas* that had developed orally beginning around 1500 B.C.E.; this religious tradition is thus sometimes also called the Vedic tradition. The Vedic religious world was one inhabited by numerous gods, or *devas*—a word related to the English word "divinity"—many of whom were personified forces of nature. Humans, although very much at the mercy and whim of these powerful beings, could nonetheless interact with and influence the *devas* by praising them and offering them sacrifices. In return, humans received boons from the gods—abundant crops, healthy sons, protection, and long lives.

A new genre of religious discourse began to emerge out of the Vedic religious world sometime between the seventh and the fifth centuries B.C.E., a body of doctrines known as the *Upanishads*. Although they would eventually become part of Hinduism, these texts—orally transmitted, like the *Vedas*—questioned the efficacy of the formal sacrifice and introduced new, essential religious ideas, many of which would eventually be adopted by the Buddha: the cyclical idea of rebirth (*samsara*), the ethical law of cause and effect (*karma*), the concept of liberation (*moksha*) from the path of asceticism, and the importance of calming the mind through meditation (*yoga*).

As the ideas of the *Upanishads* began to spread in India, some individuals, mostly men of the educated class, took them to heart, and set out to experience the liberation that these ideas described. To do so, they renounced their ties to the material world—in order to be able to focus on their spiritual pursuits—and undertook spreading these new ideas even further, and debating philosophical and meditational points. These various religious seekers were called *shramanas*—literally, "wanderers"—and the earliest Buddhists saw themselves as a subset of this general group of itinerant religious seekers. Also among these groups was Mahavira, the founder of another new religious tradition, Jainism.

At about the same time, important social changes were also in process along the Gangetic plains in northern India. Kingdoms began to emerge out of the traditional kinship structures that had governed social and political life for centuries, and with these kingdoms emerged cities and highly structured systems of government. Furthermore, trade routes began to develop between these cities, and with trade came both economic growth and the emergence of a merchant class. This latter group is particularly important in the emergence of Buddhism, for, although they had economic status, the merchants and traders did not have religious status; the Buddha would offer them a new religious path that would allow them to develop that status in part through their material support of him and his followers.

## THE VEDIC WORLDVIEW AND THE CENTRALITY
## OF SACRIFICE

The Sanskrit word *Veda* literally means "knowledge," specifically, the specialized, divinely inspired knowledge contained within the verses of these massive texts. It is a knowledge that unlocks the power of the ritual, a knowledge that is, furthermore, the special province of the Vedic priests, known as brahmins.

There are several important aspects of the *Vedas* that should be noted at the outset here. First, these were said to be revealed texts, called *shruti*—which means "heard"—by the Hindu tradition. They were said to have not been composed, but rather orally revealed to humans by the gods. The *Vedas* were thus authorless, not written but "heard" and re-membered and passed down by the brahmins. As such, they were consid-ered absolute authority, infallible truth. Furthermore, they were, and continue to be, considered by the Hindu tradition to be eternal, having always existed and forever existing, and thus were held not only to be per-fect, but also to be, essentially, religious and social imperatives, rules to be followed absolutely, without interpretation. The *Vedas*, then, and the brahmins who protected and perpetuated them—and who were the only people who could speak and hear the Vedic verses and perform the Vedic rituals—were the hallmark of Indian religious orthodoxy, and it was pre-cisely this exclusive and restricted sense of religious practice that would be challenged by the Buddha.

Perhaps because the *Vedas* were exclusively oral texts, sound (or *vac*) was considered to be the primary creative force in the world, a god (or sometimes goddess) in its own right—it is sound that unleashes the power of the sacrifice and also that which reproduces the structure of the world. Hence the *Vedas* contain verbal formulas called *mantras*, which, when re-cited, were thought to bring about creation. These formulas were in a lan-guage called "Sanskrit" (literally, "well formed"), which was the special language of the sacrifice and which embodied the properly constructed cosmos. These verbal formulas were memorized and passed down from one person to another, and only special persons—brahmin priests—could learn, speak, and hear them.

The texts that make up the *Vedas* are a mixture of hymns of praise, myths, and ritual formulas. The ritual texts, particularly the group of

liturgical texts called *Brahmanas*, present highly elaborate, often intri-
cately detailed directions for how to properly perform sacrifices to the various gods, how many bricks to use in the altars, what offerings to make
and when and by whom, and so on. Other Vedic texts, however, are directed to the many gods who control the cosmos. This, then, is a world in
which the different gods are active forces in human life and, furthermore,
in which the actions of these gods can be influenced by proper—or im-
proper, as the case may be—ritual performance. The basic goal of the
Vedic rituals was to maintain order—cosmic order among the realm of
the *devas*, and, in a parallel sense, human order. The concept of order is
indeed at the very core of the entire Hindu tradition.

The religious path expressed by the *Vedas* is one of "action," the literal
meaning of the word *karma*, and it is most fundamentally a path concerned with ritual. As such, this is a religious worldview concerned not
primarily with salvation, with what comes after this life, but with this
world—happiness, health, and wealth. Religion, in fact, was understood
in early India to be a kind of work, which when properly performed produced worldly benefits. Thus, there is in the *Vedas* an emphasis on sacrificial action, or work, and on the correct performance of that action.

The hymns of the *Vedas* were chiefly composed for chanting at sacrifices, where animals, grains, milk, and clarified butter (*ghee*) were offered
to the gods. On the most basic level, sacrifice was conceived of as a meal
offered to the *devas* by the humans. The medium of these offerings was
fire, or *agni*—both in an earthly sense (the word "agni" is related to the
English word "ignite") and in a divine sense (Agni was considered the god
of fire). Fire was essential to the Vedic religious world because it had
tremendous power: It (a) transforms the physical, material goods offered,
into "food" for the gods; (b) purifies the offerings made to the gods; (c)
represents both creative and destructive energy; and (d) is the very basis
of human domestic life (without heat and cooking, there can be no life).
Thus Agni was one of the most prominent gods in all of the *Vedas*, the
messenger between the human and the divine realm, the transporter of
the dead, and, in some verses, the embodiment of all gods. As one Vedic
verse puts it, "That which is Brahman (the whole universe, the prime
mover), the priests speak of in various forms; they call it Agni" (*Rig Veda*
1.164). Furthermore, Agni was sometimes conceived of as heat, or *tapas*,
which was also the purifying ascetic energy necessary for the proper performance of the ritual; the priests would prepare themselves for the ritual

by generating *tapas*—created through intense meditation—that burned off their spiritual impurities. As will be examined later, the Buddha took this basic idea, the purifying quality of heat, and directed it inward, rejecting the external understanding of sacrifice and making the purification process an entirely internal one.

The sacrificial world of the *Vedas* was extremely complex, involving elaborate preparations to ensure the purity of the ritual priests, the sacred space, and the sacrificial offerings. The construction of the sacrificial fire altar, likewise, involved days of careful and exacting preparations. In fact, large portions of the *Vedas* consist of highly technical instructions as to how to perform these complex rituals. Finally, the sacrifices themselves would often go on for many days, involving dozens of priests and multiple offerings to multiple gods.

In the early Vedic period, probably beginning sometime around 1500 B.C.E., the gods were considered to be the creators and preservers of the cosmos, and these *devas* were the dominant focus of the religion. Gradually, as the Vedic worldview developed over several hundred years, the religious emphasis shifted, and the centrality of the sacrifice and the sacrificial priests was emphasized more and more. Thus, in later texts such as the *Atharva Veda*, the sacrifice itself was understood to be the re-creation, on a human level, of the cosmos. Indeed, in Vedic mythology, sacrifice is what creates the world. Thus, the priests who held the special and secret knowledge of the sacrifice were seen as having the fundamental knowledge of the universe, and thus the ability to control it. They were the focus of the religious world and the sole religious actors on the religious stage. It was they and they alone who knew the sacred texts and performed the sacred rituals. Significantly, it was precisely this restricted, essentially elitist religious world—in which religious power and status was confined to a small group who inherited their positions—that the Buddha rejected and reformulated.

In addition to the ritual specialists who made up the brahmin caste, there was a subgroup of brahmins called *rishis*, or seers. On the most basic level, these were religious specialists who, through what we might call "mystical vision," were able to see into the true nature of things, into the divine realm, and thus communicate with the gods. They gained this visionary insight in part through ingesting a substance called *soma*, which gave them a purified vision. What was *soma*? The answer to this question is not known, although scholars do know that it was some sort of a hallucinogenic plant—it has been conjectured that it was perhaps the fly agaric mushroom. At any rate, *soma* was ritually prepared—there are long portions of the *Vedas* devoted to the preparation and praise of *soma*—and then ingested by the special priests as part of the larger sacrificial rituals. *Soma* is also portrayed and praised in the *Vedas* as a god, much like the Greek god Hermes—an intermediary between the world of the humans and the world of the gods.

## THE VEDIC GODS

In many respects, the early Vedic gods are personifications of natural forces—the wind, fire, rain, or sun. The gods are responsible for creation, which they effect through something called *maya*, described as the art of the gods, a projection of the gods' imaginations. The idea is that the gods give form to the powers that are already present in the cosmos, eternally, as part of the natural order of things; they do not, in this sense, create the powers, but rather make them manifest in the world. Hence, the gods are often described as craftsmen, "measurers," using their "rulers" to form the world. Thus, a prominent early Vedic god is called Vishvakarman ("maker of everything"), and he is described as the divine architect or carpenter who fashions the world out of nothing.

Prajapati ("father of life") is another Vedic creator god, described as at once the universe, time, sacrifice, and sacrificer. This is at times quite confusing: Prajapati emits all living beings via the sacrifice, and then he himself has to be put back together by the sacrifice because he himself has been sacrificed in creating the world; indeed, when the Vedic priests build the fire altar, with its 720 bricks, they are building Prajapati, who is the year (360 for the days, 360 for the nights). In this ritual, the priests are said to "reassemble" him, and the word to describe this process, not incidentally, is "sanskrit"—properly constructed, well fit. Here we can see the early articulation of a significant idea, a metaphoric rebuilding or reforming of the individual's self that gets developed in later Indian religion. The sacrifice thus not only makes the cosmos come into being, but it also, on a human level, makes the person "complete."

Another prominent Vedic god is Indra, to whom about one quarter of the verses of the *Rig Veda* are devoted. He is described as the tireless consumer of *soma*, and as the archetype of generative forces. Furthermore, it is he who creates hurricanes, who pours down rain, and who commands all forms of wetness. He is thus associated with life and, at times, destruction. Most significantly, though, he is the benevolent leader of the Aryans—the nomadic tribes who settled in northern India and who were the human authors of the *Vedas*—their great warrior and protector. Some of his epithets in the Vedic texts are the "destroyer of enemies and cities," "bestower of prosperity" on humanity, and the "lord of heaven." In significant ways, Indra, as model king, will be adopted and reformulated by the Buddhists, who will conceive of the model king not as a god but, ultimately, as the Buddha himself.

A discussion of the Vedic gods could go on for many pages, but what is important to note, in the context of the rise of Buddhism, is that the world was conceived of in these hymns and myths as being formed and ruled by powerful gods, who often, through their whimsy or divine play, reeked havoc on the human realm. Humans could certainly—via hymns of praise and sacrifice—influence the gods, but ultimately they were, in this worldview, at the mercy of these often-capricious deities. The Buddha would reject this cosmological worldview outright, and particularly this reliance on the whim of the gods, and instead would forcefully posit that humans and humans alone are responsible for their birth, their death, and, ultimately, their salvation.

## THE DYNAMICS OF CASTE

In this examination of the religious and social context out of which the Buddha and Buddhism emerged, it is important to finally consider one of the most significant aspects of Brahmanical and Vedic religious and social life against which the Buddha reacted—what is most typically called "the caste system." The Vedic religious world was hierarchical: the *devas* were at the top of this hierarchy (within the realm of the *devas* there were hierarchical divisions as well), and below them was the human realm, formally defined by the division of society into four classes, or *varnas*, membership in which was determined solely by birth. Although the caste system took many hundreds of years to develop, and was, at least initially, not so much a system—and certainly not the oppressive system that it has often been seen to be—as a means of understanding and prescribing social and religious roles, caste eventually developed into one of the defining aspects of the Hindu religious tradition.

At the top of this hierarchical social structure were the sacrificial priests, the brahmins. It was their role and duty to perform the religious rituals and to preserve and recite the *Vedas*—to memorize the thousands of verses in the texts, to chant them at the sacrificial rituals, and to pass these texts on to successive generations of brahmins orally. In so doing, the brahmins maintained the order, or *dharma*, of the divine world, assuring that the gods were appeased through sacrifice and ritual praise. Directly below the brahmins in the hierarchy were the kshatriyas, the warriors and sociopolitical rulers. Just as it was the duty of the brahmins to maintain the order of the divine world, so was it the *dharma* of the kshatriyas to preserve order in the human realm. Below the kshatriyas were the vaishyas, the cultivators and keepers of domestic animals. It was their *dharma*, accordingly, to provide food and material goods. Below them were the shudras, the laborers and servants, whose *dharma* it was to ensure the cleanliness of the other three classes of humans.

Accordingly, this was a system not only of mutual dependence, but also of restriction. There was no upward mobility in this system. One Vedic text (the *Purusha Shukta* of the *Rig Veda*) that describes the creation of the universe envisions this social system as a human being who is sacrificed to create the world: the brahmins are the mouth of the human (because of their oral preservation and performance of the sacred verses of the *Vedas*); the kshatriyas are the arms (because they are the "strong arms" of the social world); the vaishyas are the thighs (the support of the body); and, significantly, the shudras are the feet (the lowest, but also in many ways the most fundamental). Thus, social and cosmic order, *dharma*, can only be maintained if each part of the body is present and "healthy." Certainly, the feet are lower than the head, but without the feet the body cannot stand.

Although it seems that the Vedic understanding of caste bears little resemblance to the restrictive and oppressive system that later came to dominate Indian social and religious life—it was originally envisioned as a symbiotic division of labor and life—the Buddha himself was highly critical of this division of society. He saw the *jati*, or birth, model of dividing society, which was the basis of the caste system, as fundamentally oppressive, and rejected it outright. Rather, the Buddha posited that one's own effort in each life determined one's previous and future rebirths, and he also insisted that even the lowest members of the social structure could attain salvation by cultivating selfless compassion and by striving for self-awareness. Salvation, therefore, was not from a Buddhist perspective the special privilege of the brahmins, but was open to everyone.

## TIME, DEATH, AND SPECULATION IN THE LATER *VEDAS*

When the Buddha set out to find the path to enlightenment, he did so in order to conquer suffering and, ultimately, death, because he saw that it was continued rebirth—and thus also redeath—through time that was the very basis of suffering. But what was the prevailing understanding of these complex ideas at the time of the Buddha's birth?

Time was considered in the early Vedic period to be eternal; the gods and the cosmos had always existed in one form or another, and would always continue to exist. The issue of what happens to humans at death was not a prominent topic. Rather, as we have seen, it was life that was emphasized, and the sacrifice was intended to provide for matters in this world by appeasing the gods. By the late Vedic period, however, a certain note of anxiety can be detected in the Vedic discourse. The tone of the Vedic texts seems to shift, moving from the confident and remarkably unspeculative discussion of sacrifice to a troubling note of existential doubt. Questions begin to be raised about the nature of creation, about the relationship between the gods and the individual, and the very nature of death. In *Rig Veda* X (the tenth book of the *Rig Veda*), for instance, we find the question raised as to what there was in the beginning, before the world was created. Was there something, or was there nothing? What came before there was something? Does anyone know? Who created the creator? These are weighty questions, to be sure, questions that, in one form or another, are fundamental to virtually all religious traditions. Significantly, though, these questions remain unanswered in the *Vedas*, as if their human authors recognized the ultimate mysteries of the cosmos, and as if these authors wished, in the end, to invite further philosophical and existential speculation.

More specifically, the sages in the *Vedas* began to wonder whether or not there was some sort of afterlife. A kind of hell-like realm of prolonged suffering after death for those who lived poorly, who did not properly perform their religious and social duties, is sometimes discussed in the earlier texts, a realm that is overseen by the god Yama ("death"), although the nature of these hells, and how one ends up there, is generally laid out in rather vague terms. Essentially, death in the earlier *Vedas* seems to have been viewed as an inevitable end. The later texts, however, introduce the concept of a "realm of the Fathers"—somewhat mysterious figures who are, like the gods, to be praised and worshipped—where one goes after earthly death. In other words, the seeds of the concept of re-birth were sown in the later Vedic period, and by the time the *Upanishads* were introduced (about which more will be said in the following section) the fate of the individual after earthly death became a primary concern of Indian religious thought.

This marks a profound moment in the development of Indian religion, recorded in the later Vedic texts—particularly evident in the *Brahmanas*, a genre of commentarial literature that provides a kind of running inter-pretation of the *Vedas*. It is this development that would eventually lead to the emergence of Buddhism: a shift in focus is evident, away from the quid pro quo world of the sacrifice, in which offerings are made to the gods in order to get earthly results, and toward a new search for the na-ture of the self, the nature of life—indeed, a search for the very nature of existence.

## THE CHALLENGE OF THE *UPANISHADS*

This shift in focus is recorded in the *Upanishads*, a group of orally transmitted texts that began to be composed in the last part of the Vedic period, from about the eighth through the sixth centuries B.C.E. The tone of these texts is very different from that of the majority of the *Vedas*. It is existentially speculative and profoundly philosophical. It is in the *Upa-nishads* that what became the central tenets of Indian religious thought—ideas that formed the basis of Buddhist thought as well—are most clearly articulated: the concept of *samsara*, or the continuous cycle of birth, life, death, and rebirth; the idea of *atman*, a permanent self that transmigrates through *samsara* (the Buddha, however, will reject this idea of a perma-nent self); the doctrine of *karma*, moral and ethical causality; and the possibility of *moksha* (in Buddhist terms, *nirvana*) or release from this world of rebirth.

In the *Upanishads* we no longer see a model, as articulated in the *Vedas*, of a cosmos populated by a multiplicity of gods who must be influenced via the sacrifice, but rather the *Upanishads* focus on the abstract divine principle underlying all of existence, which is called *Brahman* (not to be confused with the caste *brahmin*). And what is this power? "It is the un-seen seer, the unheard hearer, the unthought thinker, the ununderstood understander. Other than It, there is no seer. Other than It, there is no hearer. Other than It, there is no thinker. Other than It, there is no understander. It is your *atman*, the inner controller, the immortal" (*Brihad Aranyaka Upanishad* 3.7.23).

The *Upanishads* are fundamentally ascetic in their orientation, advocating a religious life outside of society, a renunciation of worldy attachments. The sages who wrote them, who recorded the dialogues about the nature of the self, existence, Brahman, death, and release, rejected the Vedic involvement in things of this world. These texts locate the basic existential problem as the generation of *karma*, a word that literally means "action," but comes in the *Upanishads*—and in Buddhism as well—to refer to any intentional action that creates consequences or is performed with the anticipation of results, including, therefore, sacrificial action (which is, after all, fundamentally intended to create, to bear fruit). In order to break free from the binds of *samsara*—and it is essential to recognize that the Upanishadic sages saw rebirth as a negative phenomenon—one must find a way to stop generating *karma*, the actions that lead to rebirth, in the first place.

On its face, this may seem to be a relatively simple matter: if it is actions that create *karma*, then the solution to the existential state of human beings, to being stuck in the world of rebirth, must be the elimination of all actions. However, the Upanishadic sages recognized that it is extremely difficult to stop all actions. First, one must separate from the world of action—from sacrifice, from domestic life, from the ties of family. The *Upanishads* are thus sometimes called Forest Books, in that they advocate a simple life, removed from the hustle and bustle of the world, a life away, in the forest. Second, the *Upanishads* advocate a life of focused meditation (*yoga*) and philosophical introspection. *Yoga*, a word that literally derives from a Sanskrit verb meaning "to yoke"—as in to yoke an ox to a plow—is not understood as means to the end here. It is a mental and physical technique of concentrating on a single reality, that of Brahman, which is sometimes described in the *Upanishads* as The One, and of cultivating the realization that one's own self, one's *atman*, is no different than the divine whole of Brahman. According to the *Upanishads*, Brahman is not only the energizing force of the cosmos, but it is also the very self of the human being.

Thus, the *Upanishads* advocate a path of self-knowledge, a knowledge that results in the removal of a fundamental ignorance that creates the illusion that there is a difference between the individual *atman* and the absolute Brahman. This ignorance—which is sometimes called *maya*, or illusion—leads to grasping, to the generation of *karma*, and it is this *karma* that causes rebirth. Thus, release from the bonds of *samsara*, called *moksha*, is achieved through the elimination of ignorance about the nature of the self. One particularly illustrative dialogue, recorded in the *Katha Upanishads*, takes place between the god of death, Yama, and a brahman named Naciketas. Naciketas had won a boon from the gods, the ability to ask Yama any question he likes, so he asks the god about what happens after death: "When a man is dead, there is this doubt: Some say, 'He exists,' and some say, 'He does not exist.' I want you to instruct me in this matter." Yama, though, begs him to ask something else, saying, "Even the gods had doubt as this." But finally, after Naciketas repeatedly asks the same question, Yama instructs him, telling him that the only way to escape death, the only way to end the cycle of rebirth and attain salvation, is to "study what pertains to the self," and in the process "leave both joy and sorrow behind" (*Katha Upanishad* 1.20).

To summarize, then, the transition from the Vedic to the Upanishadic worldview is marked by a transformation of the concept of sacrifice, in which the external, formal sacrifice of the Vedic world is internalized. The outward action of the sacrifice, *karma*, is rethought and given an ethical and moral emphasis. Proper sacrifice is not in the *Upanishads* understood to be the offering up of material, into the fire of Agni, to be transported to the gods, but rather, true sacrifice is the generation of an internal heat, or *tapas*, that burns off one's desire and allows for the elimination of ignorance and, ultimately, *karma*. Furthermore, the prime religious actors of the *Upanishads* are no longer the ritual priests with their specialized knowledge of the construction of the sacrificial altar and the ritual formulas to be chanted during the sacrifice; now the religious actors are ascetics, renouncers who cultivate the knowledge of the self and, ultimately, of Brahman.

## CONCLUSION

The period during which the *Upanishads* were being formulated and eventually recorded, roughly from about 800 to 600 B.C.E., was a period of tremendous religious fermentation. Indeed, the sixth century B.C.E. in India was one in which change was happening at an extraordinarily fast rate, historically. In response to the ideas that eventually were recorded in the *Upanishads*, a diffuse group of religious seekers calling themselves *shramanas* began to reject the structured Vedic social and ritual world, and instead seek insight outside of society. The *shramanas*, then, like their Upanishadic counterparts—who, remember, were themselves brahmins— sought out the quiet of the forest and the jungle, where they could debate philosophical and religious matters among themselves, and where they could gain knowledge of their own nature, and, ultimately, of Brahman. And they felt that once they gained this understanding, they would be re- leased from the world of *samsara* and would attain eternal oneness with Brahman.

The techniques and ideas of the *shramana* movements varied consider- ably. Some advocated a harsh, extreme form of asceticism, denying them- selves any pleasure at all, sometimes to the point of rejecting all nourishment; others advocated an extreme course of meditation, in which the renouncer would, essentially, meditate at all times; and still others took the opposite extreme, and advocated a form of renunciation that looked very much like hedonism. They engaged in whatever they pleased, free of any rules or constraints. Most of these movements we know very little about, since they are only mentioned in Buddhist and Hindu sources, and only mentioned as misguided. Two, however, stand out—the Ajivakas and the Jains.

For the most part, we know of the Ajivakas only through Buddhist and Jain sources, in which they are portrayed as the archenemies of true reli- gious seekers, misguided and extreme. It is clear that they must have been very serious ascetics, practicing a much harsher ascetic course than either the Hindu renouncers or the Buddhists. To enter the Ajivaka order, for instance, one had to have all one's hair pulled out, and then grasp a molten piece of metal. Their basic doctrinal stance was that there is no human causality, really no *karma*, in the sense that it is generally known. Instead, they proposed that there was an impersonal force called *niyati*, or fate; everything in an individual's life was predestined (not by any god, just by the impersonal force of the cosmos). Humans must go through 8,400,000 *kalpas*—a *kalpa* consists of 4,320,000,000 years—being born and reborn over and over again, at the end of which we become ascetics in the final birth: "*Samsara* is measured as with a bushel, with its joy and sorrow and its appointed end. It can be neither lessened nor increased, nor is there any excess or deficiency of it. Just as a ball of thread will, when thrown, unwind to its full length, so fool and wise alike take their course, and make an end of sorrow" (*Digha Nikaya* 1.47). This was, to be sure, not a terribly attractive worldview. Not much is precisely known about the Ajivakas, and scholars do not know why the Ajivaka movement did not catch on and survive, but one thing is clear: there was no place for the laity, making it very hard for them to gain either followers or patrons (needed to provide shelter and food, especially), and without either of these, it seems that this was a self-defeating religious tradition.

In contrast to the Ajivakas, the Jains did survive and, to a degree, continue to this day to flourish in India. Jainism was founded by Vardhamana Mahavira ("the great hero"), sometimes called a Jina ("victor"), or Tirthankara (a "ford maker," who makes a crossing point out of this world), who lived at almost exactly the same time as the Buddha. Some of the basic Jain tenets include the idea that all things, including inanimate objects, contain a living force, or *jiva*, and each carries a certain karmic load. Higher forms, which have less karmic burden, also have volition, and animals and humans can affect their own *karma*. Austerity burns off *karma*. When the individual finally burns off all *karma*, he or she ascends to the realm of pure light for eternity (and the *jiva*, once there, remains individual, unlike in the Upanishadic view). Violence to other beings creates the most negative *karma*. Hence there is a real emphasis on *ahimsa*, or nonharm. Thus, Jains in India tend to be merchants, because it is one of the few trades that does not involve injuring other beings.

What is most important for the present context is to recognize that the Buddha and Buddhism arose out of this atmosphere of great religious flux, a sustained period of questioning the old religious and ritual values and practices. The Buddha certainly adopted the basic Indian religious vocabulary of his day, but he also crafted it into his own particular message, changing some basic ideas and rejecting others.

## CHAPTER 1

# THE LIFE
# OF THE BUDDHA

The Buddha's life story is really the very heart of Buddhism. Indeed, the story of the Buddha *is* the story of Buddhism. It is the orienting narrative for all Buddhists. In the language of the anthropologist Clifford Geertz, the Buddha is both a "model of" and a "model for" all Buddhists. He is not a god, but a human; he is the model of the perfect human, the perfect Buddhist. But his life does not, significantly, stand as some lofty, unattainable ideal. As such, then, his life is a model for all Buddhists, in that it is to be emulated, and, perhaps most importantly, Buddhism holds that anyone, from any position in society, can attain Buddhahood by emulating his exemplary model. Indeed, what his life story reveals is that the Buddha did not invent a new religious ideal so much as he discovered it, and he did so through his own practice. Put another way, then, he did not attain the state of spiritual enlightenment as a gift from some divine being, but rather through his own efforts, and Buddhism holds fundamentally that these efforts can, and should, be repeated by anyone who cares to reach enlightenment.

The biography of the Buddha is very complex, and at times seems contradictory, a mixture of straightforward narrative, first-person teachings, and what often seem to be flights of mythological fancy. This complexity reflects the variety of sources for his biography: doctrinal texts, dialogues recorded after his death by his followers, mythic deeds, and simple parables. Whether these various accounts of his life are fact or fiction is not really a concern for us here; rather, what is most important is to consider these sources as revealing essential points in the ongoing development of the Buddhist tradition.

## A MOST UNUSUAL BIRTH

Although Buddhism holds that the man typically referred to as "the Buddha" is one in a long lineage of enlightened beings—he is typically understood to be the twenty-fourth Buddha, the next to last, preceded by Dipankara and followed by Maitreya, whose birth will signify the end of the cosmos and the enlightenment of all beings—the overwhelming focus of early Buddhism is on the person sometimes called "the historical Buddha," that Buddha born into this particular world system.

# Buddhist Cosmology

The workings of *karma* dictate that every intentional action and thought has cumulative consequences, not only in our present life, but also in our future rebirths. Buddhist texts describe in great detail thirty-one realms or planes (typically listed in descending order and divided into three "worlds") into which beings can be reborn while still trapped in *samsara*. Each of these realms is necessarily impermanent. Thus, although those at the "top" of the cosmos are often described as utterly blissful, and rebirth there can last for aeons, eventually, all beings born there will be reborn elsewhere; likewise, beings born in the lower worlds—which include hellish births of extreme suffering, as the result of particularly negative *karma*—are eventually reborn elsewhere. Release from these realms is, as the Buddha taught, possible, but only after one has mastered the *dharma* and attained a state in which *karma* is no longer generated (this is enlightenment, or *bodhi*); for such beings, there is no further birth after death. This state of enlightenment can only be attained from the human realm. In other words, even if one is born as a god in one of the higher planes of existence, one must "fall" from that realm and be reborn into the human plane of existence in order to attain ultimate salvation, *nirvana*.

## THE IMMATERIAL WORLD (ARUPA-LOKA)

The inhabitants of the four realms that constitute this world are made up entirely of pure mind. Although they are in the highest of the realms, relatively conceived, because they have no physical bodies, they cannot hear the Buddha's teachings and must eventually be reborn in the lower human realm in order to obtain enlightenment.

31. Neither Perception nor Nonperception

30. Nothingness

29. Infinite Consciousness

28. Infinite Space

## THE FINE MATERIAL WORLD (RUPA-LOKA)

The first five realms in this world are called the Pure Abodes (*suddhavasa*); they are accessible only to those who have attained a very high degree of religious progress: nonreturners and arhats. Further down in this realm are reborn beings of lesser, although still significant, spiritual attainment. All these realms are characterized as blissful states of meditation and joy.

27. Peerless *Devas*

26. Clear-sighted *Devas*

25. Beautiful *Devas*

24. Untroubled *Devas*

23. *Devas* not Falling

22. Unconscious Beings

21. Very Fruitful *Devas*

20. *Devas* of Refulgent Glory

19. *Devas* of Unbounded Glory

18. *Devas* of Limited Glory

17. *Devas* of Streaming Radiance

16. *Devas* of Unbounded Radiance

15. *Devas* of Limited Radiance

14. Great Brahmas

13. Ministers of Brahma

12. Retinue of Brahma

## THE SENSUOUS WORLD (KAMA-LOKA)

The last seven realms in this world are called Pleasant, and include the
realm of the lesser gods (including Mara, the god of delusion and death), as
well as the realm of human beings. In the realm of Contented *Devas*, the
"Tushita" realm, *bodhisattvas* are reborn before their final human birth, after which they attain *nirvana*. Significantly, *nirvana* can only be attained
from the human realm, because it is only in this realm that the realities of
*samsara* and suffering can be fully understood and transcended.

11. *Devas* Wielding Power over the Creation of Others

10. *Devas* Delighting in Creation

9. Contented *Devas*

8. Yama *Devas*

7. The Thirty-three Gods

6. *Devas* of the Four Great Kings

5. Human Beings

4. Asuras

3. Hungry Ghosts

2. Animals

1. Hell

The Buddhist tradition holds that the man who would eventually become known as the Buddha was born near what is now the border between Nepal and India, in a small village called Lumbini. Although there
has been considerable debate as to the exact dates of his birth and death,
the Buddha seems to have lived in the middle of the fifth century B.C.E.
Importantly, though, the Buddha's life story does not really begin there,
but with the stories of his many prior births, stories that emphasize the
development of the particular moral and ethical qualities that the fully
enlightened Buddha would eventually perfectly embody. In some of these
stories the Buddha-to-be is an animal; in others he is a god; and in still
others he is a human. These prior lives are recorded in what are known as
the *Jatakas*, a canonical collection of 547 stories that vary considerably in
both length and detail.

In one of the most well known of these stories, the "Vessantara Jataka," the Buddha-to-be is in his penultimate birth, a *bodhisattva* (in this context, simply a being destined for enlightenment) named Vessantara, a prince who gives away his entire kingdom out of selfless generosity (in later Buddhist literature, Vessantara is celebrated as the embodiment of perfect giving). When Vessantara dies, he is then reborn as a divine being in the Tushita heaven, where he waits for the time to be right until he is eventually reborn, this time as Siddhartha, a prince who becomes the Buddha.

## THE BIRTH OF THE BUDDHA

The Buddha was born into a kshatriya family, and thus he was a member of the caste of warriors and kings, and, importantly, not a member of the brahmin caste, the group of religious specialists in the Hindu tradition. His family were members of a clan called the Shakyas, and he was given the name Siddhartha ("he whose goal will be accomplished") Gautama, although he is also referred to later as "Shakyamuni" (the "sage of the Shakyas"). This multiplicity of names can at times be confusing, since he is alternately called simply "the Buddha," "Shakyamuni," "Siddhartha," and "Gautama." Although he was not born into a brahmin family, it was from the start clear that Siddhartha would be an extraordinary human being, a man destined for greatness.

First, the Buddha's conception was immaculate, a detail that is not dwelled upon in later Buddhist texts, but which, at the very least, marks the young Siddhartha as a particularly special person, one who is also not tainted by the impurity associated with sexual activity in Indian thought. According to the early Buddhist tradition, the Buddha's mother, Mahamaya, dreamed that a white elephant—a standard symbol in Indian literature for royal power—entered her womb and implanted a fetus there. She then discovered that she was, in fact, pregnant. Upon learning of his wife's unusual impregnation, Siddhartha's father, the king of a small state, summoned his royal sages to interpret the significance of his wife's puzzling dream. They predicted that the child would be a boy, and that he would be destined for greatness—either he would inherit his father's kingdom and become a great ruler (called a *Cakkavattin* in Pali, *Cakravartin* in Sanskrit) or he would leave his home and family and become a great religious leader (a *buddha*, or "an enlightened one").

This aura of majesty and mysterious destiny is further emphasized in the basic outline of the story, recorded in several early Buddhist texts, of the Buddha's actual birth. In the final stages of her pregnancy, Mahamaya traveled to visit her family, and en route went into labor, giving birth to Siddhartha in a grove of trees near the humble village of Lumbini. In the standard depiction of this scene—in literary sources as well as sculptures and paintings—Mahamaya stands with one arm holding a low-hanging branch of a tree, and Siddhartha emerges from the womb, frequently diving out of his mother's side, spotlessly pure. He is caught by a group of attendant *devas* (divine beings), often in a pure cloth or, sometimes, in a golden net. But the miraculous oddity of his birth does not end there: the baby, who is typically depicted more like a young boy than like a newborn, turns in each of the cardinal directions, determines that he is the foremost of all beings in the world, and then takes seven steps toward the east (the auspicious direction, which he will also face at the time of his enlightenment), and proclaims that he is the chief of the world. Certainly, this miraculous birth and the superhuman acts of this newborn may seem to be purely mythical. However, these feats are intended by the Buddhist tradition to emphasize the special qualities and powers of this most exalted of all persons.

## PALACE LIFE

The young prince's mother died only a week after his birth. This is a detail that will become particularly significant after he attains enlightenment, because he magically transports himself to the realm of the Thirty-three Gods, where his mother has been reborn. There he preaches to her in order that she, too, can attain enlightenment. At any rate, Siddhartha is thus raised by his father's second wife, his mother's sister. All of the various accounts of Siddhartha's early life emphasize the luxury of the young prince's upbringing. On one level, the opulence and privilege of life in the palace are appropriate to a royal context in India. On another level, however, the lavish surroundings of his early life stand in sharp contrast to the asceticism he will later embrace; the texts thus emphasize, through a considerable degree of overstatement, the dangers and distractions of material life and, perhaps more importantly, the effort it takes to leave such distractions behind. But there is more to the narrative of the Buddha's youth: because of the prediction of the sages, his father, Shuddhodana, kept him confined to the palace grounds, worried that he would take the predicted course of a renouncer rather than that of a great ruler. Indeed, the king made sure that young Siddhartha could see and experience only sweetness and light. In one sermon, delivered shortly after his enlightenment, the Buddha describes his childhood in this way:

> *Bhikkhus* [monks], I was delicately nurtured, exceedingly delicately nurtured, delicately nurtured beyond measure. In my father's residence lotus-ponds were made: one of blue lotuses, one of red and another of white lotuses, just for my sake. . . . My turban was made of Kashi cloth [silk from modern Varanasi], as was my jacket, my tunic, and my cloak. . . . I had three palaces: one for winter, one for summer and one for the rainy season. . . . In the rainy season palace, during the four months of the rains, I was entertained only by female musicians, and I did not come down from the palace. (*Anguttara Nikaya*)

Within the confines of the palace, Siddhartha lived, essentially, a normal Brahmanical life, one appropriate to his royal status. He was being groomed to eventually become king: he thus passed from the student stage, in which he learned the tenets of the religion and the fundamental principles of kingship, to the beginnings of the householder stage. He married a beautiful young woman named Yashodhara, and at twenty-nine fathered a child, named Rahula. There is an intentional emphasis in the various biographical sources on the Buddha's life experience: although he did, to be sure, lead a sheltered life, he also experienced the full spectrum of human life, including the emotional attachments one forms with a wife and child.

The early texts describe the young prince's move to renunciation in various ways. Some portray it as a gradual realization of the suffering inherent in life, a slow awakening to his destiny. Others, however, emphasize his awakening to the illusory nature of his sheltered life, and to the harsh reality of the world outside of the palace, as a sudden realization. For instance, in the *Nidanakatha*, a later commentarial text, the young prince's awareness of the suffering outside of the palace walls is described as a series of visions. Although his father had labored to remove all unpleasantness from the confines of the palace walls, the gods conspired to enlighten the prince, to reveal to him the true nature of existence. It is significant that it is the *devas* who do this: the gods of Hinduism, too, from a Buddhist perspective, are trapped in *samsara*, and thus are in need of the Buddha's teachings, just as much as humans are.

## ENCOUNTERING SUFFERING

In perhaps the most widely repeated version of the story, one day the young prince persuaded his chariot driver, Chandaka, to take him outside of the gates of the marvelous palace his father had made for him, and there—out in the real world—he saw the first of four things that would transform his life. He saw an old man, and, puzzled at this "strange" human, he asked his driver: "Good charioteer, who is this man with white hair, supporting himself on the staff in his hand, with his eyes veiled by the brows, and his limbs relaxed and bent? Is this some transformation in him, or his original state, or mere chance?" The driver answered that it was old age, and the prince asked, "Will this evil come upon me also?" (See Document 1). The answer to the prince's question was, of course, yes.

On two subsequent trips outside of the palace, Siddhartha saw a diseased man and then a dead man, and on each occasion had much the same discussion with the driver. These visions represent Shakyamuni's first encounter with suffering, with *dukkha*, and the experience transforms the happy prince into a brooding young man. As Ashvaghosha's *Buddhacarita* (Life of the Buddha) 3.34, written several hundred years after the Buddha's death, puts it, "[H]e was perturbed in his lofty soul at hearing of old age, like a bull on hearing the crash of a thunderbolt nearby." He wondered if perhaps this luxurious palace life was all there was to life, whether it was truly real. He wondered what the nature of this suffering was, what its cause was, and, ultimately, what its antidote might be. He stumbled about the palace grounds in a profound existential crisis.

The fourth thing he saw, though, on his last trip outside the walls with his charioteer, was a wandering ascetic. Having encountered not only the *dukkha*—sometimes translated as "suffering," but really "dissatisfaction"—that characterizes the world but also, in the ascetic, a potential way out of this realm of suffering, he began to wonder if perhaps this life as a good kshatriya son, husband, and father was not the proper course for him.

When he returned to the palace after this last trip, he was surrounded by beautiful women dancing and playing enchanting music for him. He drifted off to sleep, and when he woke up, he found all of the women asleep around him: he found them in every manner of disarray, some snoring, others drooling, some grinding their teeth, some revealing what should be hidden, looking like so many corpses piled together. In other words, he realized that what in one context seems like youth and beauty looks like decay and squalor in another. Thus, as with the insight he gained from the first three visions—old age, sickness, and death—he realized that the world is not what it seems on the surface, and that, in fact, like the makeup that the women wear, or the artificial cleanliness of the palace, the appearance of things masks their true nature. At this moment, then, he resolved to leave the palace and go out into the world and wander in search of the truth.

## DEPARTURE

The story goes that Siddhartha snuck out of the palace while everyone was asleep, first going to his sleeping father to whisper to him that he was leaving not out of lack of respect for him, nor out of his own selfishness, but because he had a profound desire to liberate the world from old age and death, from the fear of suffering that comes with old age and death—in short, from suffering. He also went to see his sleeping wife and newborn son—and here, the significance of the boy's name, Rahula, "the fetter," is particularly poignant. Although he was torn by the sight of the sleeping infant, as any parent would be, he resisted the urge to pick him up, knowing that the feel of the boy in his arms would weaken his resolve. Instead, he resolved to return once he attained enlightenment and share it with his son. He then fled the palace on horseback and set off to find the path to salvation.

Many of the texts that narrate this story take pains to emphasize not only the internal struggle of the young prince, but also the sorrow caused by his departure. In a particularly poignant and poetic image, Ashvaghosha, in his *Buddhacarita*, says that Yashodhara, upon hearing that her husband had renounced his domestic life, had left her and her young child, "fell upon the ground, like a Brahmani duck without its mate," a reference to the beautiful brown ducks that are said to mate for life, and which, in Indian love poetry, are the very embodiment of true, enduring love—if one mate dies, the other is said to perish from a broken heart.

Although at first blush this emphasis on the emotional effects of Siddhartha's renunciation may seem paradoxical, these texts emphasize the almost heroic effort it takes to renounce the world; as for the pain and anguish left in the wake of his departure, this seems to emphasize the seriousness of the renouncer's charge. Yes, there will be those who suffer in the short term—the Buddha's wife and child, his father, the common people who would have been his subjects had he become a Cakravartin. But this short-term suffering is a small price to pay for the ultimate liberation of the entire world.

## THE BUDDHA'S ENLIGHTENMENT

The canonical texts portray Siddhartha's decision to leave the palace in a variety of ways, although they generally emphasize that this was not a sudden, rash decision, but one that gradually developed through careful and thoughtful consideration of the *dukkha* that characterizes existence, and the difficulty of escaping this suffering while still remaining involved in the world. In the *Majjhima Nikaya*, for instance, the young prince, just prior to his departure, states this difficulty quite clearly: "House life is crowded and dusty; going forth is wide open. It is not easy, living life in a household, to lead a holy-life as utterly perfect as a polished shell. Suppose I were to shave off my hair and beard, put on saffron garments, and go forth from home into homelessness?" (*Majjhima Nikaya* 1.36.12). This simple realization, an affirmation of the ascetic path, became the basic template for all future Buddhist renouncers: in order to attain equanimity of mind, which is necessary to remove the bonds of attachment that give rise to suffering, one must separate from society. This separation is called "renunciation" in Buddhism, and the way it is stated is particularly telling: to become a monk, one "goes from home to homelessness."

Siddhartha's quest for enlightenment led him first to the loosely structured *shramana* community that had formed in northern India. He first encountered two teachers whom the texts name as Alara Kalama and Udraka Ramaputra, and from them he received various spiritual insights and teachings, particularly meditational techniques and a basic yogic vocabulary consistent with that worked out in the Hindu *Upanishads*. From Alara Kalama he quickly learned to enter a meditational state of calm described as the "sphere of nothingness." Shakyamuni realized, though, that this was only a temporary state of equanimity, and not the enlightenment that he was seeking, and so he left Alara Kalama and took up study with Udraka Ramaputra. This time, Siddhartha quickly perfected a meditational state called the "sphere of neither perception nor nonperception," a blissfully calm state of mental equipoise. Again, however, he rejected this state as temporary, and therefore not the permanent state of enlightenment that he was seeking. In other words, what he sought was not temporary relief from the *dukkha* of the world; rather, he wanted a permanent antidote to the ills of the world.

He thus set out on his own path, and was quickly joined by five other *shramanas*. Together they began a course of extremely rigorous asceticism. Siddhartha applied himself with great effort to this radical lifestyle for six years; he perfected controlling his breath to the point that he suffered terrible headaches, stomach pains, and a burning sensation throughout his body; he practiced fasting, to the point that he could sit in meditation for many days on end, barely eating. The narratives of his life story say that he got to the point that he could exist on a single sesame seed a day, then on one grain of rice, then on only one jujube. Eventually, he reached a state in which he was barely breathing, barely alive.

> Because of so little nourishment, all my limbs became like some withered creepers with knotted joints; my buttocks like a buffalo's hoof; my back-bone protruding like a string of balls; my ribs like rafters of a dilapidated shed; the pupils of my eyes appeared sunk deep in their sockets as water appears shining at the bottom of a deep well; my scalp became shriveled and shrunk as a bitter gourd cut unripe becomes shriveled and shrunk by sun and wind . . . the skin of my belly came to be cleaving to my back-bone; when I wanted to obey the calls of nature, I fell down on my face then and there; when I stroked my limbs with my hand, hairs rotted at the roots fell away from my body. (*Majjhima Nikaya*)

He realized at this point that this could not be the way to enlightenment and abandoned these extreme ascetic practices, with the thought "Might there still be another path to awakening?" (*Majjhima Nikaya* 1.36.30). He then remembered a passing moment in his childhood when he had slipped into a state of utter calm and equilibrium while watching a plow. He realized with this vision of a simple, mundane moment that rather than extreme asceticism, which could only lead to more suffering, he must return to this simple moment of calm, and thereby forge a middle path between the extreme asceticism that he had been practicing and the sensual indulgence of his former life in the palace.

Siddhartha's fellow *shramanas* abandoned him at this point. They cursed and ridiculed him, denouncing him as weak willed. He was thus left alone, emaciated and sapped of all physical and mental energy. A passing woman named Sujata, however, offered him a bowl of rice gruel, and with this modest nourishment Siddhartha sat down beneath a ficus tree, facing east, near the town of Gaya along the banks of the Phalgu River, and vowed not to rise until he had reached his goal of true enlightenment. He made rapid progress.

In the middle of his meditations, however, he was challenged by an evil superhuman named Mara. Mara stands in Buddhist literature and art as the embodiment of temptations of all kinds, fear, delusion, and death, a being who would, as Buddhism became established, become perhaps the most well known emblem of *dukkha*. First, Mara attempted to plant doubt in Siddhartha's mind, and then sent his ten armies—an array of demons who represented the basis for illusion and grasping in the world, as well as hunger, thirst, craving, sexual desire, sloth, fear, and so on. Siddhartha defeated them simply by recognizing them for what they were. In later versions of the story, Mara then unleashed his daughters, lustful and voluptuous temptresses, in whom Siddhartha showed not even the slightest interest. Finally, Mara challenged Siddhartha's very right to enlightenment—if he was who he said he was, then who in the cosmos could prove this? In one of the most famous images in all of Buddhism, reproduced in countless sculptures—an iconographic form known as the *bhumisparsha mudra*, or "earth touching gesture"—Shakyamuni reached out with one hand, as he was meditating, and touched the earth, at which point the goddess of the earth bore witness to his right to the throne of enlightenment by creating a tremendous rumbling and shaking, and by making an ocean flow from her hair. Mara, terrified at this awesome display—and realizing that this man, the Buddha, was indeed about to realize his goal, was indeed about to conquer death—gathered his armies of illusion and lust, and fled, thoroughly defeated.

Siddhartha's path to enlightenment was then clear of any remaining obstacles, and he made rapid progress, meditating through the night, which, in the canonical accounts, was divided into three periods, or "watches." In the first, he attained knowledge of his past lives; in the second, he gained the power to see the past lives of other beings; and in the third, he attained insight into the causally conditioned nature of reality. As the sun rose, he achieved the state of perfect omniscience (in Pali, *bodhi*) and was, at this point, fully enlightened—the Buddha, the Awakened One.

After his awakening, at the age of thirty-five, the Buddha spent seven weeks at Bodhgaya, in the vicinity of the Bodhi tree, meditating on the various aspects of the truth, or *dharma*, that he had realized. He was initially hesitant to share his teachings, however, for he felt that the complexity of his meditational vision would be too hard for humans to grasp, and would, in fact, lead to further confusion and suffering: "I have realized this Truth which is deep, difficult to see, difficult to understand . . . comprehensible by the wise. Men who are overpowered by passion and surrounded by a mass of darkness cannot see this Truth which is against the current, which is lofty, deep, subtle and hard to comprehend" (*Majjhima Nikaya* 1.26.19).

At this point, according to the tradition, the gods—frequently Brahma himself, the Hindu god who is often called "the Creator"—came to him to convince him to accept his vocation as teacher, appealing to his compassion and assuring him that in fact there were people capable of understanding the *dharma*. One used the image of a lotus pond: in a lotus pond there are some lotuses still under water; there are others that have risen only up to the water level; and there are still others that stand above water and are untouched by it. In a similar way, in this world there are people of different levels of development. Thus challenged, the Buddha determined to proclaim the insight he had gained. Initially, he wished to preach to his first two teachers, Alara Kalama and Udraka Ramaputra, but the gods informed him that they had both died. He thus decided to share his insight with the ascetics who were his early companions—the very ones who had rejected him—and set out on foot for the Deer Park in Isipatana (modern Sarnath), where he would offer his first discourse on the *dharma*.

---

## CONCLUSION

The Buddha's first "sermon," then, was given to the very ascetics who had earlier abandoned him during his meditations. It was a gesture of the Buddha's selfless compassion—he recognized that these ascetics, who had dismissed him for giving up too easily, were earnest but misguided in their efforts to find enlightenment, and so he sought them out first to set them on the correct path, the "middle path" between the extreme asceticism in which they were engaged and the hedonism that he himself had experienced in the palace. They gathered around him and he spoke what is known as the First Turning of the Wheel of *Dharma*, in which he laid out the basic outline of his knowledge and experience of enlightenment to these five ascetics. This first discourse represents, in many ways, the beginning of Buddhism, since it is with the sharing of his personal religious experience that the Buddha really created Buddhism.

Tradition maintains that the content of that first sermon, which will be explored in the next chapter, was so powerful that these five disciples quickly—after a week—attained enlightenment, becoming *arhats*, or "worthy beings." These first five followers, in turn, went forth and began to teach the *dharma* that the Buddha had shared with them. This was the beginning of the Buddhist *sangha*, the community and institution of monks that is at the heart of the religion.

Among the many aspects of the Buddha's life story that stand out and that became central to the Buddhist tradition as it developed in India and beyond, two bear particular note. First, in the many versions of his life, it is consistently emphasized that the Buddha was not a god, but a human, and a human not from the highest rank of society. Thus, his life was to serve as the basic model for all future Buddhists. Second, the *dharma* was not divinely bestowed, but discovered, and discovered through an examination of the Buddha's own life experience. In other words, although one may not be born, like Siddhartha, as a kshatriya and may not, like Siddhartha, be marked from birth as an extraordinary human being, anyone, regardless of birth or status, can attain this same state of enlightenment.

## CHAPTER 2

# THE ESTABLISHMENT OF BUDDHISM IN INDIA

## TURNING THE WHEEL OF *DHARMA*

Initially, the five ascetics with whom the Buddha had earlier practiced were reluctant to listen to anything that the newly enlightened Buddha had to say, regarding him as a weak-willed backslider. He had, after all, abandoned them and their ascetic practices. However, as they listened to him and absorbed the power of his spiritual transformation, their resolve dissolved, and they saluted him and offered him a special seat before them. This set the stage for the Buddha's first sermon. He began by telling them that he was no longer to be called "Siddhartha," but now was the Tathagata (the "thus gone one," which refers to his enlightened state), an *arhat* (one worthy of respect), a perfectly enlightened being, and that he will share with them the insight that has allowed him to conquer death.

The first sermon—the *Dharmacakrapravartana Sutra*, "the *sutra* of the turning of the wheel of *dharma*"—is one of the best known of all Buddhist texts (See Document 4). It is both an extremely straightforward discourse and an extremely persuasive one. It is simple in structure and language, and lays out the foundation of all Buddhism. The Buddha begins by telling the ascetics who will become his first disciples, and therefore the first Buddhists, that the truth he has discovered is a middle path between extremes. At one end of the spectrum is the very sort of asceticism that he gained firsthand experience of, an extreme asceticism that amounts to, essentially, useless self-torture. At the other end is sexual and sensual indulgence, which simply leads to more grasping and, therefore, more suffering. The middle path, he says, leads to self-knowledge, equanimity, awakening, and, ultimately, salvation (*nirvana*).

The Buddha then lays out what is really the doctrinal foundation of

Buddhism, the Four Noble Truths. This set of four truths is really a kind of basic blueprint, a kind of fundamental summation of the insight that the Buddha had gained in his enlightenment experience. Although Buddhist doctrine would become extremely complex as the tradition develops and as different schools—with different philosophical positions—emerged, each articulating increasingly intricate analyses of consciousness, perception, cognition, psychological states, and so on, the Four Noble Truths would remain the doctrinal bedrock of Buddhism.

The first noble truth posits that suffering exists in the world. This we see in the story of Siddhartha in the palace: the young prince is made aware that the world is not all wonderful—as it appears to be in the palace—but in fact that the rosy life is just an illusion. In his first sermon, the Buddha says that birth is *dukkha*, old age is *dukkha*, sickness is *dukkha*, death is *dukkha*; in fact, everything is suffering, including things that seem to be pleasurable. But *dukkha* is more than this: it is really the truth of the physical and mental discomfort that comes from not getting what one wants, or, conversely, from getting what one does not most wish for. Pleasurable experiences, for instance, engender suffering because they necessarily do not last, and so, when the experience is over, one is dissatisfied because one wishes for more.

It is important to note, however, that the first noble truth is not intended to engender a pessimistic worldview in Buddhists, but rather to alert them to the reality of the world and to promote a clear, truthful view of that world—to see it as being, essentially, in a constant state of flux and change. Furthermore, the response to the reality of suffering, as is clearly evident in the Buddha's own desire to realize and share the *dharma*, is not existential despair, but the cultivation of compassion (*karuna*) and kindness (*maitri*) to all living beings.

The second noble truth is the arising (*samudaya*) of suffering, which is fundamentally related to the basic Buddhist understanding of *karma* (see below), of cause and effect. Since suffering exists, the Buddha posits, it must have a cause, which is most simply expressed as *tanha*, thirst or desire. This thirst takes many forms: the desire for life, for things, for love. Although on its face this, too, may seem to engender a pessimistic worldview, in which the individual must stifle all sensual pleasures, it is important, again, to stress that the Buddha advocates a middle path, between sensual indulgence and extreme asceticism. Pleasurable experiences should be experienced for what they are, without grasping. Indeed, the

Buddha pronounces that it is precisely because humans mindlessly grasp things and experiences, always rushing to the next, that they fail to fully experience their lives, including that which is pleasurable. The point, then, is not to deny the sensual, but to fully experience sensations and thoughts, as they are happening.

Since suffering has a beginning, the Buddha posits, it must, logically, also have an ending: the third noble truth, then, is the cessation (*nirodha*) of suffering. The end of *dukkha* is related to its source; *nirodha* comes as a result of ending craving, of stopping the grasping after things that are imperma-nent. When one stops grasping, one stops generating *karma*, and it is *karma* and *karma* alone that keeps beings trapped in *samsara*. The absolute elimi-nation of *karma* is *nirvana*, eternal freedom from the bondage of *samsara*.

Of all Buddhist concepts, *nirvana* has perhaps been the most misunder-stood. Although it is frequently equated with heaven, or described as a state of bliss, *nirvana* is actually the absence of all states. This Sanskrit word lit-erally means, "to extinguish," as one would snuff out a candle. Since *karma* is what keeps us in *samsara*, what constitutes our very being, the elimina-tion of *karma* logically means elimination of being. This is the end of *dukkha*, the end of the cycle of birth, life, death, and rebirth, beyond all states of existence. When the Buddha died, then, when his physical body expired, he did not "go" to *nirvana*, but rather ceased to exist, absolutely.

Despite the fact that *nirvana* is the Buddhist understanding of ultimate salvation, the Buddha himself had little to say on the topic, often warn-ing his followers of the dangers of grasping on to the end goal at the ex-pense of living a focused, compassionate life. He describes it as "the extinction of desire, the extinction of illusion," and also as the "aban-doning and destruction of desire and craving . . . that is the cessation of *dukkha*." However, when asked once if *nirvana* were a state of existence or not, the Buddha responded that this was an unanswerable question, and left it at that. The point is that the focus should be on mindful progres-sion on the path, not on the destination. The person who spends too much time obsessively focusing on *nirvana*—or on any aspect of existence or doctrinal complexity—is, the Buddha said, like a man who, upon being shot by a poisoned arrow, asks who shot it, how he aimed, what sort of wood it was made of, and so on. The man must first remove the arrow before the poison kills him.

That said, however, later Buddhist schools inevitably took up the question of *nirvana*, frequently engaging in long philosophical analyses of the possibility of describing it in positive terms, and in some Mahayana schools, which emerged sometime around the first century C.E., *nirvana* is, in fact, often described as a kind of state of blissful calm.

Finally, the fourth noble truth is the existence of an eightfold path (*marga*, or *magga* in Pali) to religious realization, which consists of

1. Right understanding

2. Right intentions

3. Right speech

4. Right action

5. Right livelihood

6. Right effort

7. Right mindfulness

8. Right concentration

On one level, this is a set of sequentially arranged steps: one must move from the first step on the path, Right understanding, to the final step, Right concentration. At the end of this path lies enlightenment, the conquering of suffering and death—*nirvana*. However, the Buddha also stresses that each of these steps must be embodied continually. In other words, one does not so much move from one step to the next, but moves through them sequentially, always practicing what was mastered in the previous step.

The Eightfold Path is really a kind of practical overview of the path to enlightenment. The path is traditionally divided into three distinct phases, sometimes called "trainings," that should, ideally, be progressively mastered. The first is *shila*, or ethics, and involves purifying one's outward behavior (and motivations for such behavior). This is the first stage on the path because it is considered impossible to purify one's mind without first purifying one's actions. The Buddha describes three elements in *shila*: right action, right speech, and right livelihood. Next comes *samadhi*, or meditation, which is broken down, likewise, into three elements (the next three steps on the path): right effort, right mindfulness, and right concentration. The third phase is *prajna*, or wisdom, and is broken up into right understanding and right intentions.

Translating *prajna* as wisdom, however, is a bit misleading, because it is not just knowledge or things that one learns. Rather, it is a profound way of understanding being in the world. *Prajna* is often described as a sword that cuts through all illusion, a mental faculty that enables one to fully experience the world as it is, without grasping. A later school uses an image of geese reflected on a perfectly still pond to describe this state. The average person looks at the pond, and, upon seeing the reflection of a flock of geese, immediately looks up. But the person who has perfected *prajna* does not look up, but rather fully experiences the thing that he or she is seeing at the moment, the reality of the reflection, without distractions. In a sense, such a person does not think at all, but only sees the world as it is—as what the Buddha called *yathabhutam*—in a state of perpetual flux.

In the end, then, the Four Noble Truths, as laid out by the Buddha in his first sermon, present a remarkably clear summary of the doctrinal foundations of Buddhism.

## CENTRAL DOCTRINES OF BUDDHISM

As Buddhism gained followers, and monks began to form distinct groups, often united on the basis of doctrinal commonalities and matters of monastic discipline, Buddhism was marked by what really was a kind of doctrinal explosion. Over the course of the first few hundred years after the Buddha's death, and particularly at the beginning of the first few centuries of the Common Era, substantial new texts began to appear: commentaries on the Buddha's sermons, texts devoted to monastic life, and entirely new texts claimed to have been hidden by the Buddha himself, which offered up philosophical and devotional ideas that seemed to move very far from the Buddha's original teachings. This doctrinal profusion is truly one of the hallmarks of Buddhism (some of the highlights of these doctrinal developments will be explored in more detail in a later chapter). This said, however, there are certain key doctrines shared by all Buddhists:

*Samsara.* Underlying virtually all of Buddhism is the doctrine of *samsara*, which Buddhism shares with Hinduism. *Samsara* is really a fundamental worldview or ethos, an understanding of the world, which holds that all beings, including animals, are part of an endless (and beginningless) cycle of birth, life, death, and rebirth. Furthermore, Buddhism holds that the physical universe is itself made up of infinite world systems, spread out infinitely in space, and that these world systems, like the individual person, are also subject to the cycle of birth and rebirth. It was, in many ways, the realization of the horror of *samsara* that led to the *Upanishads* and the *shramana* movements—attempts to find a way out of this endless cycle of rebirth.

The Buddhist view of the cosmos is predicated on *samsara*, and holds, as seen in Chapter 1, that there are both different world systems and also different realms that are arranged in a tripartite structure—the "sense-desire" realm at the bottom, above which is the "pure form" realm, and at the top, the "formless" realm. Within these three divisions are sub-realms into which a being can be reborn: the human realm, animal realm, hungry ghost (*preta*) realm, various hells, and, higher up, deva (divine) realms. Although it is not the highest realm, the human realm is considered the most promising because in this realm there is both suffering, which acts as a motivation to advance, and free will, which enables humans to act on this impulse. It is important to note here that Buddhism holds that even the divine beings, despite their power, are subject to the laws of *samsara*.

*Karma*. This term literally means "act" or "deed," and is, as noted in Chapter 1, a concept shared with Hinduism. *Karma* is the linchpin of the whole religious system, in that it is *karma* that determines the quality of each rebirth, and also that which keeps the individual in *samsara*. On its most basic level, *karma* is the natural law of cause and effect, inherent in the very structure of the world, a cumulative system in which good acts produce good results, and bad acts, bad results. Beings are then reborn in good or bad realms, depending on their cumulative *karma* in each birth. *Karma* is frequently described in Buddhist texts as being a seed, or *phalam*, which will eventually grow fruit, the quality and abundance of which is, naturally, dependent on what sort of seed was sown.

The Buddhist understanding of *karma*, though, further stipulates that it is not just the act that determines the karmic result, but also the motivation behind the act. Thus, good acts done for the wrong reason produce negative karmic results, and, likewise, bad acts that might have been done for good reasons (or accidentally) do not necessarily produce negative karmic results. Indeed, Buddhism holds that bad thoughts are every bit as detrimental as bad actions.

Negative *karma* is most typically created through intentionally harming other beings and through greed. Likewise, positive *karma* is most easily created through compassionate acts and thoughts and through giving selflessly (which is, ultimately, motivated by compassion).

*Impermanence.* The doctrine of impermanence, or *anitya*, is rooted in the three visions that prompted Siddhartha to abandon his life in the palace. What he realized, when he saw old age, disease, and death, is that all beings are in a fundamental state of flux and, ultimately, decay. This is, in an important sense, a basic corollary to the reality of *samsara*—the human being, just as the world, is constantly evolving, decaying, and reforming. Furthermore, it is due to the failure to recognize this flux that beings suffer, because they grasp on to that which is impermanent—life, love, material objects, and so on—wishing it will last. The Buddha condenses this basic idea in a simple pronouncement: "Whatever is impermanent is suffering." Since everything is necessarily impermanent, then everything, ultimately, involves suffering, which he succinctly expresses in the phrase *sarvam dukkham*, "everything is suffering."

*No Self.* The doctrine of no self, or *anatman*, is frequently misunderstood in the West. The Buddha does not mean that human beings have no personality, but rather that because everything in the world is impermanent, there can be no permanent self. In this way, Buddhism significantly breaks from Hindu doctrine, which holds that there does exist a permanent self that is reborn time and time again in *samsara*. But if there is no permanent self, what is it that is reborn? Karmic residue alone. In his second sermon, the Buddha explains that what we think of as "the self " is only a collection of personality traits, or *khandas*. They create the impression that there are both objects to be perceived and a person to perceive the objects, when in fact all of these objects are impermanent, constantly changing.

One of the clearest expressions of this basic Buddhist idea is contained in a conversation between the monk Nagasena and King Milinda, from the Pali text *Milindapanha* (See Document 12). Nagasena uses the example of a chariot to illustrate no self, pointing out to Milinda that although one can point to, see, and ride a chariot, it only exists in so far as it is a collection of parts—axles, wheels, reins, and so on—and that since no single part can be called "the chariot," there is no essential, independent thing called a chariot, just as there is no essential, independent self.

*Conditioned Arising, or Pratityasamutpada.* This is often called the "chain of becoming," which is broken into twelve links, and is one of the most important Buddhist doctrines. About this, the Buddha's disciple Sariputta says, "Whoever understands conditioned arising understands the *dharma*." This is a more elaborate understanding of *karma* and *samsara*, a vision of cause and effect in which everything in the world is dependent on some other thing for its existence, and is succinctly expressed in this simple formula: "When this is, that is / This arising, that arises / When this is not, that is not / This ceasing, that ceases." In other words, one thing begets another. Birth begets life, which begets decay, which begets death, which begets birth, and around and around. To get out of the circle, the chain must be broken somewhere, most efficiently at its weakest link, ignorance, which is done by applying oneself to mastering the *dharma*.

## THE FORMATION OF THE MONASTIC COMMUNITY

After his enlightenment, the Buddha traveled almost without stop throughout India for the next forty years, sharing the *dharma* and gathering followers. He did, however, stay in one place for three months out of every year, during the monsoon season. This period, known later as the "rain season retreat," became an essential element in the formation not only of Buddhist monasticism, but also of the Buddhist lay community. Monks settled in small communities throughout India, debating amongst themselves, establishing a formal religious canon and an accepted body of religious practices, and sharing the Buddha's teachings with the laypeople. The laity, in turn, supported the monks materially by providing them with shelter, food, robes, and alms bowls.

Toward the end of his life, the Buddha instructed his followers that no single person or group of people could hold authority over the community of monks and laypersons. Rather, the authority was to be shared by all, and was to be based on the *dharma* that he had taught. In one of the most emotionally powerful moments in all of Buddhism, recorded in the *Mahaparinirvana Sutra*, the Buddha makes this point to his chief disciple and companion, Ananda.

At the age of eighty, the Buddha decided, having made known his *dharma* completely, to pass out of this world in three months' time. Ananda, who had been his faithful companion for forty years, learned that his teacher's death was imminent, and was distraught. Indeed, in some versions of the story, Ananda is beside himself with grief, found alone in the monastery, desolate, sobbing. The Buddha called him and asked why he was so sad, and Ananda replied: "Alas! I am still but a learner, one who has more work to do. And the Teacher is about to pass away from me—he who is so compassionate to me!" Ananda here is expressing several layers of distress, not the least of which is the sheer emotion of losing a dear companion. What is perhaps most emphasized in the passage, though, is Ananda's fear that without the present Buddha there to teach and guide him, he will have no chance to attain *nirvana*. The Buddha, however, assures him that he has left the teachings, the *dharma*, and that is all that one needs. He tells Ananda that he and all the other monks must now be "lights unto themselves," by which he means that the *dharma* is there to guide them, but they and they only are responsible for their spiritual progress.

The earliest community of monks, the *sangha*, was initially the assembly of the Buddha's immediate disciples and was a loosely knit group of ascetics who lived a simple life focused on understanding—and, as the following paragraph shows, remembering—the Buddha's teachings, and on practicing meditation. From what the early texts say, these early monks required very little to live: a set of robes (traditionally made out of discarded cloth) and a needle for sewing them, a begging bowl, a belt, a razor for shaving their heads, a water strainer (to prevent the accidental ingestion of insects, which, because it involves harming another living being, would lead to the generation of negative *karma*), and a walking staff. They lived a life of wandering, modeled on the Buddha himself, moving from town to town in order to prevent personal and emotional attachments, begging for their sustenance and, in return, offering up discussions of the Buddha's teachings.

In the early decades after the Buddha's death, before his teachings were committed to writing, the monks must have made great efforts to memorize these teachings. They did so by systematically organizing the teachings into groups, which were eventually gathered into three sets of what the tradition regards as the Buddha's actual words—although it is doubtful that any of the texts are not marked by embellishment. These are known collectively as the *Tripitaka*: the Discipline (*Vinaya*), Teachings (*Sutra*), and Advanced Doctrine (*Abhidharma*). As these collections were being formed orally, though, frequent debates arose among the different groups of monks as to both the contents of these discourses as well as their significance. Furthermore, new situations, which had not been explicitly addressed by the Buddha, arose, leading to the need for new rules, which also led to disagreements. Thus, as much as the idea that the Buddha's teachings were the ultimate authority created a fundamentally egalitarian religious community, it also, after the Buddha's death, opened the way for both productive debate and disagreement about the meaning and significance of the teachings that he had left behind.

These debates often led to schisms within the community, which were resolved in a series of councils. In fact, according to tradition, the Buddha himself had anticipated such scenarios:

> O *Bhikkhus*, as long as you remain united and meet together frequently, so long the *Sangha* will continue to flourish and prosper. So long as you meet together and decide all important questions in union and harmony one with another, and do not make new and oppressive rules, hard to keep, where I have made none, but strictly adhere to the observance of those rules which I have given you for your help and protection—so long as you do this, the *Sangha* will never decay and die out. (*Digha Nikaya* 16.6)

The tradition records that shortly after the Buddha's death, the first of these councils was held in the town of Rajagriha (Rajgir in modern Bihar) to discuss issues of doctrine and practice. In particular, some monks had begun to complain that the disciplinary rules described by the Buddha were too strict, the life he proposed too austere. In one account, a monk named Subbhada is said to have remarked, "Enough your Reverences, do not grieve, do not lament. We are well rid of this great recluse [the Buddha] We were tormented when he said, '[T]his is allowable to you, this is not allowable to you[,]' but now we will be able to do as we like and we will not have to do what we do not like." The elder monk Mahakashyapa, overhearing the discontented young monk's words, called a meeting of the monks to address this and other issues, and they met—five hundred are said to have gathered—during the three-month period in the rainy season.

First, Mahakashyapa addressed a long series of questions to the monk Upali, an expert in monastic discipline, or *Vinaya*. His answers to these questions, which Upali had remembered (according to the tradition, exactly as the Buddha himself had spoken them), make up the *Vinaya Pitaka*, the "basket" of monastic rules and regulations. These were initially memorized by the monks and preserved orally, until they were eventually written down (it is difficult to date this, but it would seem that this happened no earlier than the first century C.E.). This task—memorizing the *Vinaya*—must have been epic in nature, as the collection, in written form, runs hundreds of pages in length.

Mahakashyapa then addressed another series of questions to Ananda, who proceeded to recite in order each of the *nikayas*, the long "chapters," that make up the second of the collections, the *Sutra Pitaka*, and are largely concerned with issues of the *dharma*. Ananda, who was the constant companion of the Buddha, is said to have heard each of his master's *dharma* talks firsthand, and so each of these texts—sometimes referred to as "sermons," since they are *dharma* talks delivered by the Buddha on various occasions—begins with the standard Pali phrase *evam me sutam*, "thus have I heard."

Another council was held about a century later, again, to address issues of monastic discipline—a group of monks in western India, the Sthaviras ("the elders") learned that monks in the east were making changes in the monastic rules. At this council, held in the eastern city of Vaishali, the Sthaviras argued that although minor changes in the rules could be made, based on one's teachers' interpretations, the *Vinaya* was the ultimate authority and should, when possible, serve as the monastic guideline. The eastern monks did not agree. As a result of these disagreements over proper monastic behavior—and also over the doctrinal principles that were necessarily involved—the *sangha* eventually divided into two different lines of monastic ordination, the Elders (Sthavira) and the Great Assembly (Mahasamghika). Although the differences between these two groups initially mostly revolved around issues of monastic discipline, or *Vinaya*, more fundamental differences in doctrine and practice would eventually develop. These two groups—and there were other subgroups as well, some of which had their own, often very complex, understandings of doctrine and practice—would eventually become the Theravada (the "doctrine of the elders") and the Mahayana (the "great vehicle").

## MONASTIC LIFE

Although much of the *Vinaya* is concerned with monastic discipline and proper responses to disciplinary transgressions, it is also a rich source of information about the life of early Buddhist monks. Although permanent monasteries became common as the Buddhist tradition became more established in India, in the first few centuries after the Buddha's death, the life of the monk was one of wandering; indeed, the Pali term for "becoming a monk" is *pabajja*, "to go forth." The standard way of saying one had become a monk in the texts was to say he had "gone forth from home to homelessness." The ideal monk spent much of his time in meditation, alone, under a tree or in a cave, although the monk was cautioned not to be too remote. Indeed, monks seemed to remain relatively near villages and towns for one simple reason: they were dependent on laypeople for their sustenance, and to go too far away from human settlements was to risk starvation.

The solitary life of the wanderer was considered by the early tradition to be the most conducive to progress on the Path, precisely because it was free from distractions and allowed for the cultivation of nonattachment, but the wandering life out in the open became extremely difficult during the monsoons. In Buddhist texts, this is typically referred to as the "rainy season," and because travel was so difficult during this period, the monks, following the model of the Buddha, tended to gather together during this period in temporary dwellings, often donated by wealthy lay patrons. This would have been a period of relative rest, certainly, and also a time for discussions about doctrinal issues, meditational techniques, and so on. Gradually, over the first few centuries after the Buddha's death, these temporary dwellings became more established, and served as the basis for the first permanent Buddhist monasteries in India.

The formation of permanent monastic communities created in early Buddhism a basic monastic division, between those monks who settled in the monasteries (referred to in the texts as town monks) and those who continued to live as wanderers (forest monks), a division that continues to the present day. Town-dwelling monks were much more involved not only in the day-to-day activities of the monastery, but also in the life of the laypeople as well. Such monks performed a number of services for the lay community. They taught the *dharma* and instructed them in the fundamentals of the religious tradition; they provided the opportunity for giving, an essential part of lay Buddhist religious life, by serving as a pure field of merit; and they often officiated at funerals. (See Chapter 3 for more on this topic.)

In contrast, forest monks, who are sometimes referred to as "meditation-duty monks," lived a much simpler, much more secluded, life, focused on meditation and learning the fine points of the *dharma*. Ironically, because they were seen as being more ascetically rigorous than their village counterparts, they were frequently perceived by the laity as being purer, and thus more worthy of donations. Therefore, the very thing these monks wished to avoid—involvement with the material world— came to them in the form of gifts donated by laypeople wishing to generate greater merit by giving to a purer merit field.

In early Buddhism, there were also female monks, or nuns (the Pali word *Bhikkhuni* is simply a feminine version of the word for monk). The Buddha reluctantly admitted women into the *sangha* after his own aunt, Mahaprajapati Gautami, entreated him, with the help of Ananda, to allow for the formation of a female order. There were stricter rules for female monks, and they had extra rules; they were also considered subordinate to male monks. This is no doubt a reflection of the basic view about women in India at the time. That said, however, it is perhaps surprising that a religion that was so radically egalitarian in its understanding of who can obtain salvation—remember, the Buddha said that one must be "one's own light," and that salvation was entirely a matter of self-effort—would have relegated women to what essentially amounted to a kind of second-class citizenship. And, although the female monastic orders seems to have been well established in the early period, by the second or third century C.E., the order appears to have all but died out, and the role of women became largely a lay affair.

## CHAPTER 3

# THE EXPANSION OF BUDDHISM IN INDIA

The religious world into which the Buddha was born was one character-ized by an unprecedented philosophical effervescence. The Buddha re-sponded to this changing climate and was also a significant cause of change. The period after the Buddha's death was also one of tremendous change; just as the intellectual and religious world was rapidly shifting, so too was the socioeconomic world. This chapter explores the social and political conditions that facilitated not only the survival of this new reli-gion, but also its rapid expansion within India and, eventually, beyond its borders.

## AN URBAN EXPLOSION

Buddhism arose in an environment of competing ascetic movements. The majority of these movements seem to have faded away almost as soon as they emerged; indeed, only Buddhism and Jainism continued to attract significant numbers of followers after the death of their founders. One group of ascetics who achieved a degree of prominence in this mi-lieu, the Ajivakas, are known only through Buddhist and Jain texts. Al-though this sect seems to have survived until the thirteenth century, the Ajivakas never gained a substantial following, owing in no small part to the extreme nature of their religious message. The Ajivakas were, at least from the Buddhist perspective, rigidly fatalistic, adopting a strictly deter-minist understanding of the religious path. According to them, essen-tially, no human effort could have any effect against fate, or *niyati*. Salvation, which was understood simply as an end to all human exis-tence, could be reached only after living through an immense number of lives, which proceeded automatically like the unwinding of a ball of thread, the last life being as an Ajivaka monk. And the life of these monks was one of extreme deprivation. No human effort could have any effect on the process. It was, therefore, extremely difficult for the Aji-vakas not only to attract followers and converts, but also to attract lay supporters, since no act of giving to the Ajivaka monks would have any positive effect on the donor.

This, then, points to an extremely important aspect of Buddhism that was fundamental to its survival and expansion in India, namely, its appeal to lay supporters. One element that seems to have enabled Buddhism to survive and prosper as a new religious movement was the dynamics of *dana*, religious giving. Through giving to the monks, the layperson could accumulate positive *karma*, which, in turn, would enable him or her to as-cend the karmic scale; the monks, in turn, not only served as a fertile karmic field in which the layperson's gift would bear positive karmic fruit, but also received the material support—the layperson's gift—that en-abled them to survive. There was more to the equation than this, though, for one of the factors that facilitated Buddhist expansion in India seems to be that Buddhism was particularly well suited to the changing social and political environment of early India. It may also be the case, how-ever, that as much as Buddhism provided an antidote to this changing so-cial climate and the anxieties, it also contributed to it.

The centuries immediately before and after the Buddha's birth saw the rapid growth of cities in northern India, which brought with it a whole range of major changes. One historian of India has characterized the broad effect of urbanization as a "spiritual malaise."[1] First, the shift from a rural, agricultural life to an urban, trade-based life—a shift that took place in India from about the sixth to the third centuries B.C.E.—would have necessitated a complex division of labor and the development of specialized professional groups. This change in economic organization, in turn, would have led to a shift in social organization, such that the famil-ial organization of the rural village would gradually have given way to trade- and labor-based social grouping. This may, indeed, be reflected in

---

1. Richard Gombrich, *Theravada Buddhism: A Social History from Ancient Benares to Modern Colombo* (London: Routledge and Kegan Paul, 1988), 57.

the emergent caste system, which is, after all, a social order based fundamentally on occupation.

Urbanization also led to greater social freedom and mobility, which, in
turn, would have necessitated the emergence of an increasingly complex
bureaucracy to keep the population in check. Indeed, it is precisely this
changing social structure that the Buddhist text *Aganna Sutta* seems to reflect: it is, on one level, a myth of the origin of the world, but a number of
scholars have seen in it a social and political commentary reflective of a
changing, and sometimes chaotic, society.

Although some Buddhist texts do decry city life as too crowded and
chaotic to be conducive to religious progress, and Buddhism is fundamentally an ascetically oriented religious tradition that favors a life outside of
society, in significant respects, Buddhism was at least implicitly more ac-
cepting of some of the specific challenges of urban life than the Brahmanism that preceded it. For instance, within the confines of the city,
there would have been communal eating places—in part to facilitate the
influx of workers without families from the outlying rural areas. The
Brahmanical social structure, as embodied in the caste system, with its
elaborate rules regarding diet and intercaste contact, would not have permitted such communal dining. Buddhism, in contrast, does not adhere to
these social distinctions, and so, communal dining would have posed no
religious hurdles. Likewise, communal religious gatherings in the urban
setting would not, for the Buddhists, have posed a problem, whereas for
the Brahmanical religious adherents they would have been fraught with
potential pollution. We could add to this list a whole range of urban social conditions to which Buddhism was well adapted, from the use of
money in trade to the existence of brothels.

It would certainly be an overstatement to claim that laypersons converted
to Buddhism only because it better suited the social conditions of the newly
emergent urban world. The issue is far more complex than this. But it does
seem likely that Buddhism thrived in these new cities in part because it was
better suited than Brahmanism, Jainism, or any of the other religious traditions of the period to the particular demands of urban life. It allowed for the
intermingling of disparate social groups; it provided a religious orientation
that permitted, if not actually encourage, social mobility; and it embraced,
quite explicitly, persons from what would have been the lower echelons of
the brahmanical social order—laborers, traders, merchants, and kings.

## BUDDHISM AND TRADE

Another important factor in the establishment and growth of Buddhism in India was the emergence of important trade routes across northern India, for instance, the famous Silk Route, but also lesser known roads as well as river travel. The traders who traveled along these routes brought with them every manner of material goods, and this influx of goods—and the ability to transport goods to other regions—was instrumental in the growth of cities. Another important dimension of this growth in trade, however, was that it enabled Buddhists and Buddhism to spread first within India, and then, rapidly, outside of the Indian subcontinent.

There are frequent references in early Buddhist literature to trade and traders, caravans, guilds of merchants, and the market towns that sprung up along major trade routes. In the *Vinaya*, for instance, the Buddha encounters and interacts with a caravan leader named Blattha Kaccana, who was going along with five hundred wagons filled with jars of sugar; likewise, caravans are mentioned in several of the *Jatakas*. Although it is impossible to determine exactly why these and other texts so frequently make mention of traders, they seem to be reflective of a close tie between Buddhism and trade. Monks certainly traveled with these caravans and seem to have occasionally spent the rainy season with these traders, as evinced in a text, in which the Buddha explicitly gives a monk permission to do so. On the surface, this makes sense, since Buddhism, with its rejection of the caste system, would have welcomed traders and merchants as converts. Furthermore, as we have already seen, because Buddhism espoused that there was a karmic benefit to giving, especially giving of wealth to monks, there may have been a particular incentive on the part of merchants and traders to support Buddhism.

Furthermore, travel was very dangerous, and lone monks would have faced the perils of weather, disease, wilderness, and bandits. In the company of a caravan, however, a monk would have been afforded a degree of safety and physical comfort. There is significant textual and archaeological evidence that monks who set off to spread the *dharma* after the Buddha's death followed established trade routes. In the *Sutta Nipata*, for instance, a monk and his disciples journey from northern India to the Deccan plains and into the Krishna River valley (which is in the modern state of Andhra Pradesh) following an itinerary that is clearly a trade route. And the great temple at Amaravati in southern India, as well as other significant monasteries and temples throughout India, was obviously located along the important trade route of the Krishna River. This was in part because river travel would have allowed for the transportation of building material, and also because river trade would have allowed for an influx of pilgrims and patrons.

## THE RISE OF MONASTERIES

The earliest Buddhist monks were, as we have seen, wanderers, living in no fixed location. Indeed, this was an essential component of the life of the monk: to live with no attachments, material or emotional. However, it soon became clear that these wandering monks would need shelter, particularly during the monsoon season. The earliest versions of monasteries were simple cave dwellings. Such dwellings, however simple, had to have been donated and maintained by lay and royal patrons. Thus, from the very beginning, monasteries involved a symbiosis between the monk and the layperson: monks needed the layperson's material support and shelter; the layperson needed the monk to share the Buddha's teachings and to provide a field of merit.

Significantly, monasteries also were a place of shelter for traders and merchants, and many of the earliest monasteries sprang up along trade routes. These merchants and traders provided, as noted above, the money and goods to sustain monastic life, while the merchants received in return not only the Buddhist *dharma*, but also physical haven. Furthermore, as cities rapidly grew along the Ganges Valley, the merchants who populated these cities invited monks to establish monasteries there, thus allowing the merchants opportunities for merit making.

Relatively soon after the Buddha's death, two distinct forms of monastic establishments emerged—village monasteries and forest hermitages. In the village monasteries—which were typically located on the fringes of cities, despite the name—the monks had a great deal of contact with their lay supporters. Monks in these monasteries were intimately involved in the daily life of the town, functioning as teachers, preachers of the *dharma*, and even doctors. In this way, the monks could effectively spread the teachings and practices of Buddhism by at once involving the laity in the life of the monastery and, at the same time, themselves becoming involved in the life of the village or town. However, there were inherent dangers in this symbiosis.

Monks were not prohibited from the possession of property. They took no vow of poverty. However, the *Vinaya* and other texts make it abundantly clear that the monk was to keep his or her possessions to a minimum, to those objects—begging bowl, robes, toothbrush, and so on—that were necessary for comfortable, but not lavish, living. The dynamics of giving, *dana*, however are such that giving more can seem to be karmically beneficial. Because wealthier laypersons wished to earn more merit by giving more, monks and monasteries were sometimes given large tracts of land, servants, lavish personal goods, and so on. All of these were considered to be hindrances to the monk's individual progress on the Buddhist path, in that they represented precisely the material trappings and attachments that the monastic life was, after all, intended to avoid.

The solution to this dilemma proved to be rather simple: such gifts were to be treated as the communal property of the monastery. However, although this may have solved the immediate problem of the individual monk becoming too attached to material possessions, it also led to another, larger problem, namely, the monastery as large landholder. Indeed, monasteries were sometimes extremely wealthy institutions, and their maintenance involved the employment of hundreds of workers and the development of an increasingly large and complex internal bureaucracy. Furthermore, one of the paradoxes of the increasing wealth of these monasteries—a wealth that came about, after all, because of the gifts from laypersons wishing to earn positive *karma*—was the perception that the monks had become corrupted by such lavish living, and that the field of merit was no longer pure. An important ritual thus developed, the *Pratimoksha* (in Pali, *Patimokkha*) ceremony, which served to maintain the internal purity of the monastery while at the same time assuring the laity that the monks were not becoming corrupted.

As recorded in the *Vinaya*, the Buddha is said to have prescribed that on each full moon and new moon days all the monks in residence in a single monastery must come together in a formal meeting. If at least four *bhikkhus* can be assembled, then they should listen to the full list of 227 *Pratimoksha* rules contained within the *Vinaya*. Before the ritual recitation begins, however, each *bhikkhu* should formally and openly admit to any offences that he (or, in the case of a female monastic order, she) knows he has committed. Once this free admittance of a transgression has been made, the monk is considered "pure" and can listen to the recitation of the rules.

Forest monks led a markedly different life than those of their village counterparts. Because they were removed from virtually all contact with the lay community, they did not serve either as fields of merit for the laity's gifts or as teachers of the *dharma*. Rather, they were much freer to spend their time in meditation and ascetic practices.

Early Buddhist texts do not discuss these two varieties of monastic life as standing in opposition to one another, although occasional conflicts did seem to arise, such as that which prompted the second Buddhist council, discussed in Chapter 2. Indeed, it seems that any given monk would have passed back and forth between forest and village monastic life. And, although it may seem on the surface that it was the village or town monks who were most responsible for the spread of Buddhism after the Buddha's death, the forest monks were also instrumental in the expansion of Buddhism, in that they not only cultivated advanced meditational techniques, but also shared the basics of meditational practice with both the village monks and, indirectly, the laity. Furthermore, because the forest dweller tended to engage in more austere ascetic practices, and thus was in some sense a more pure object of giving, the presence of these monks in the village and town monasteries, upon their return from the forest, would have added a special degree of purity to the monastic community.

The ideal monk of the early Buddhist community, as reflected in several Buddhist texts, seems to have been one who combined the more socially active role of the village monk with that of the meditational and ascetic practices of the forest monk. Following the model of the Buddha, such a monk would have begun the day with a period of isolated meditation. Then he would have put on his robes, taken up his alms bowl, and gone out to ask for sustenance from the lay community. Having eaten, the monk would then have shared a *dharma* lesson with the laypeople. He would then have returned to the quiet of the monastery to meditate. Finally, toward the end of the day, the monks of the monastery would have come together as a group, to hear *dharma* instructions from a senior monk. This lesson would then have been followed by a period of meditation before sleep.

## ASHOKA THE DHARMA KING

Buddhist texts are full of references to kings and rulers. First, there are the images in the Buddha's own life story: he was destined, the sages said at his birth, to become either a great world ruler, a *cakravartin*, or a world renouncer. Thus, from the outset, Buddhism had a special appeal to kings and others in the political realm, and there can be little doubt that without royal support, Buddhism would never have survived as a religious tradition. This may, in large part, be due to the simple fact that the status of the king was decidedly ambiguous in ancient India. The king obviously wielded tremendous political power, what we might call "real" power—commanding armies, gathering taxes, owning property, making and enforcing laws, and so on. He was always lower in religious status than the brahmins, and in some ways subservient to the priestly caste. Because kings necessarily engaged in actions that harmed other living beings, such as waging war and quelling dissent, they were seen in brahmanical terms as karmically tainted.

The Buddha himself was from a royal family, and thus a kshatriya by birth. Although he rejected this caste identity when he renounced the world, it may be that he felt a special personal regard for kings and other political figures. One of his most important early patrons was the king of Magadha, Bimbisara, whose capitol was located at Rajagriha. According to the "Pabbaja Sutta" of the *Sutta Nipata* commentary, Bimbisara first saw the ascetic Siddhartha through his palace window and, curious as to his identity, went out to find him. He invited Siddhartha to visit his court, but Shakyamuni declined; however, he promised to return once he had attained enlightenment. When the Buddha and his disciples visited Rajagriha after the enlightenment, they were entertained as royal guests. In a famous scene, Bimbisara poured water from a golden jar onto the Buddha's hands to express his adherence to the Buddha's teachings, and gave him and the *sangha* the gift of Veluvana Park—or Vulture's Peak as it is more commonly known—and promised to continue to patronize Buddhism and promote its growth.

Another very important king in early Buddhist literature is Milinda (also known as Menander or Menandros), a Greco-Bactrian who reigned over what is now modern Afghanistan and northern India, in the latter half of the second century B.C.E. Milinda is best known for the series of discussions he had with the Buddhist monk Nagasena, which were compiled into the famous work entitled *Milindapanha* (See Document 12). Although in many ways Milinda serves as a foil for Nagasena, providing an opportunity for an extended examination of the *dharma*, he is also portrayed as a wise and compassionate king and, importantly, as a supporter of Buddhism.

Certainly, the most important king in the Buddhist world, and one of the most important figures in the entire history of Buddhism, is Ashoka (273–232 B.C.E.), the ruler of what became the largest empire in India's history. Not only did Ashoka become a Buddhist himself, but he also established a model of dharmic kingship that would remain the standard template for all Buddhist rulers to follow. Furthermore, Ashoka was instrumental in the growth and expansion of Buddhism. He erected numerous large stone pillars throughout India with edicts inscribed on them, edicts that laid out many of the basic aspects of the Buddha's teachings as well as guidelines for how to live a good Buddhist life. He also established the standard of royal support for the monks by building monastic shelters, planting trees and digging wells to aid travelers, and spreading the physical remains of the Buddha throughout India. Enshrined in *chaityas* and *stupas*—burial mounds of varying sizes—these remains became objects of devotion and important gathering places, often associated with significant events in the Buddha's life, allowing the monks to spread the *dharma* to larger and larger groups. Ashoka also sent out a number of missionaries, including one led by his own son, Mahinda, to introduce Buddhism and establish monastic orders in other parts of the world, including Sri Lanka, Southwest and Southeast Asia, and even Greece.

We know about Ashoka through two sources: the inscriptions that he left throughout India, and Buddhist mytho-history—semi-historical chronicles such as the *Dipavamsa*, *Mahavamsa*, and the *Ashoka Avadana*. Ashoka's grandfather, Chandragupta, founded the Mauryan empire, the largest India had to that point ever known, covering northern India from the Bay of Bengal to the Arabian Sea. We know little about Ashoka's father, Bindusara, except that he further expanded Chandragupta's empire into southern India, as far south as the Deccan Plateau. Although there is some debate on the matter, Ashoka seems to have ascended the throne in 268 B.C.E.

By all accounts, Ashoka—or as he was called in his inscriptions, Devanampiya Piyadasi, "he who is looked on with affection, the beloved of the gods"—was a great warrior, brave, fearless, and mighty. According to later Buddhist sources, however, Ashoka was an ugly young man, and he is portrayed as being intensely disliked by his father. In these sources, the pre-Buddhist Ashoka is portrayed as a truly nasty fellow; indeed, he is called "chanda Ashoka," which translates as "cruel Ashoka," and sometimes "kama Ashoka," or "Ashoka the lustful." He is said to have had many brothers (sometimes as many as ninety-nine), and his desire to become the king was so strong, the texts say, that he had several of these brothers killed (sometimes all but one of them) in order to inherit his father's kingdom. These sources go to great lengths to emphasize the negative aspects of Ashoka's character prior to his conversion to Buddhism. For instance, one source recounts a story in which Ashoka was once playfully teased by some women in his harem and he had them burned at a stake for their offence. He is described as being a ruthless torturer of wrongdoers, quick and harsh to punish; he had a state prison built that came to be known as "hell" by his subjects. He was also a man with a marked proclivity for war.

Although upon the death of his father Ashoka became the ruler of a kingdom that covered a huge expanse of land, almost the whole of India, he was not satisfied. According to the Buddhist chronicles, he wanted more land, more money, more power, and so, eight years after his coronation, he initiated a bloody siege against the neighboring Kalingans, who lived in what is now modern Orissa in the far northeast of India. It was a horrible, bloody war, a war in which thousands and thousands of lives were lost, in which brothers turned against brothers, sons against fathers, and for every atrocity committed there was a reprisal that took the carnage a step further. In the end, though, Devanampiya and his armies prevailed. But looking out at his newly conquered lands, at the bloody battlefields, the thousands of slaughtered soldiers from both sides, and the thousands of innocents killed, the king was filled not with a sense of gain and victory, but with a profound sense of loss, an unbearable remorse. This sense of grief is expressed in one of the inscriptions that Ashoka left behind:

> Devanampiya feels sorrow at having conquered the Kalingans. Indeed, the conquest of a previously unconquered country, which involves killing, dying, and deportation, still impresses itself upon Devanampiya and weighs heavily on his mind. But this depresses him even more: Living in Kalinga, there were brahmins and recluses, adherents of other sects, and householders who practiced obedience to elders and to their parents and teachers, who behaved courteously

toward friends, acquaintances, companions, relatives, slaves, and servants, and who were devout. They were all injured or killed or separated from those who were dear to them. Even those who themselves were lucky enough to escape harm were affected by the afflictions of their friends, acquaintances, companions, and relatives. And this weighs heavily on the mind of Devanampiya: all people share in this suffering. For there is no country . . . where there are no brahmins or recluses, and there is no country where there are people who do not feel some sort of faith. Even if the number of people who were killed in Kalinga, who died, or were deported had been a hundred or a thousand times less, this would still weigh heavily on the mind of Devanampiya.

Ashoka responded to this event in a profound way—he converted to Buddhism.

According to the edicts, Ashoka first became a Buddhist layperson, an *upasaka*. It seems, however, that he did not make sufficient progress on the path as a casual Buddhist. Desiring more knowledge of the *dharma*, he then, according to one inscription, "went to the *Sangha*." Although it is not entirely clear what this reference means, it would seem that he went to the monks directly and received extensive teaching from them in a monastic setting. This is an extremely important point, for it establishes a basic model of the king as a kind of pupil of the monk. Indeed, in order for the king to rule properly, dharmically, it was necessary for him to receive such teachings from the *sangha*. That said, however, it is important to note that the *dharma* of Ashoka's edicts is in no way a detailed excursus on the Buddha's teachings. Rather, the *dharma* put forth is a kind of sweeping righteousness, a basic set of moral and ethical guidelines with which to live and, for the king, to govern. It is clear, however, that the Buddha's teachings fundamentally informed Ashoka and his radical reforms.

In the edicts, Ashoka lays out a sweeping set of ethical guidelines. He pledges his support for all religions and religious peoples in his realm, and pronounces religious tolerance to be the rule in his kingdom. He establishes monasteries and shelters for ascetics, digs wells for pilgrims, and plants trees for shade and shelter. He also extols the virtue of the simple ascetic life. He encourages his subjects to respect and care for the elderly and to treat their servants with dignity. He promotes an approach to life based on the principle of nonviolence and puts severe limits on sacrifices.

This latter point, although on one level a simple advocacy of a kind of basic karmic harmony, is particularly important in terms of Ashoka's support of Buddhism. Although he does not outright state it, this limiting of what can be offered sacrificially seems to be intentionally targeted at the brahmin priests: without animals to offer up to the gods, they could not perform their basic religious duties. Thus, although he explicitly promotes tolerance of all religious groups, we can see in Ashoka's edicts a subtle but very real move to limit the influence of the brahmins. By advocating Buddhism, Ashoka would have subverted the basic brahmanical hierarchy—since Buddhism does not recognize the spiritual superiority of any particular group of people based on birth—and in the process asserted the status of the righteous, dharmic king as not only a political leader, but also a religious leader.

The edicts talk of Ashoka going on a *Dharma Yatra*, a pilgrimage to the important sites associated with the life of the Buddha. He starts at Bodhgaya, the place of the Buddha's enlightenment, and then proceeds to Lumbini. This, too, is an extremely important moment in the expansion of Buddhism because these physical places become, in later Buddhism, centers of the Buddha's teachings, pilgrimage destinations for Buddhists not just living in India, but also elsewhere in the rapidly expanding Buddhist world. Bodhgaya, for instance, in part because of Ashoka's early visit to the site, becomes a kind of Buddhist Jerusalem or Mecca, the birthplace of the religion, a physical reminder of the continued presence and relevance of the Buddha's salvific message and path.

Because he had his edicts inscribed on stone pillars and slabs throughout his realm, across the whole of India, Ashoka was able to very effectively spread the teachings of the Buddha, and at the same time establish the legitimacy of his own dharmic political rule across an incredibly large expanse of land. But perhaps his most lasting and far-reaching contributions to the history of Buddhism were the missions that he sent out from India, for it is they who allowed Buddhism to expand beyond its homeland and develop into the world religion that it is today.

The edicts make mention of missions only once, stating that emissaries were sent out to five other kings and to several other kingdoms; it is not clear, however, based on the inscriptions, whether these were truly religious missions or were primarily political in nature. It may well be that this distinction was not a meaningful one in the third century B.C.E. It is, however, in later Buddhist sources, particularly in the great chronicles from Sri Lanka—the *Dipavamsa* and the *Mahavamsa*—that Ashoka's missions are most celebrated and most elaborately discussed. Certainly, these sources are not completely accurate as historical documents, and tend toward exaggeration when discussing Ashoka's deeds, but they present, nonetheless, a great deal of information about the development and spread of Buddhism.

These chronicles describe a schism within the monastic community: unorthodox sects had taken up residence in the monasteries, which led to clashes on issues of monastic discipline and proper ascetic practices. According to some sources, these clashes turned violent, and some monks were actually killed. Ashoka intervened and purged the monasteries of the impure monks. He then held a council—the third Buddhist council, according to the sources—in his palace at Pataliputra, where the disciplinary issues were resolved and, according to the Buddhist chronicles, the Buddhist Canon was completed. It was at this point, according to the later chronicles, that he sent out groups of monks to spread the Buddha's teachings.

The chronicles tell us that Ashoka sent his son off on the first Buddhist mission, to the island of Sri Lanka, just off the southern tip of India. Mahinda took with him a layperson and four monks, the latter so that there would be a group of five monks who would be able, in accordance with *Vinaya* rules, to confer higher ordination on any young man who wished to become a monk. The accounts of Mahinda's mission in the chronicles—which contain many miraculous details—say that the first person the monks met was the king of the island, Devanampiyatissa. He was a king with whom Ashoka had already established a relationship, according to some later sources, who immediately converted to Buddhism and then donated the land for the first monastery to be built on the island. Mahinda had also brought with him a branch of the Bodhi tree from Bodhgaya, the tree under which the Buddha had attained enlightenment, to plant in the monastery. Although the historical veracity of this story may be questionable, the event establishes the ubiquity of the Bodhi tree as a symbol of the Buddha and Buddhism—virtually all Buddhist monasteries and temples, throughout the world, have at their center a Bodhi tree.

Regardless of the specific historical accuracy of the chronicles' accounts of Ashoka's missions and his specifically Buddhist activities—it is important to remember that these texts were written either by or for

Buddhist monks, and so are intended to emphasize the religious significance of historical events—what is important is that Ashoka established
the principle that Buddhism is a missionizing religious tradition, and that
the king, as the model lay Buddhist, supports and promotes the *sangha*'s
missionizing activities. These texts thus stress the close relationship between the *sangha* and the king.

## CHAPTER 4

# THE CONTINUED PRESENCE OF THE BUDDHA

Buddhism is most typically portrayed as a religion of the mind, one that eschews ritual and physical worship. Certainly, it can be concluded that Buddhism took root in India and spread primarily because of the power of the Buddha's teachings. However, there was more to the equation than this: to emerge from the context of competing religious sects along the Ganges, and to spread throughout India and eventually into other parts of Asia, it was necessary that Buddhism was supported, by laypeople and by political rulers. It was not, however, only the words of the Buddha that spread—it was also his personality and his physical image. This chapter explores the ways in which Buddhists preserved the presence of the Buddha in physical objects, such as relics and artistic images.

## BE YOUR OWN LIGHT

One of the most basic elements of the Buddha's teachings, indeed the very basis of the *dharma*, is self-reliance for progress on the Path. The law of karmic cause and effect makes it clear that the only thing that can effect one's religious progress is one's own efforts at meditation and introspection. No gods are there to intercede. Although the monks do provide instructions and guidance, they cannot intervene in any way. Put simply, it is up to the individual to follow the teachings and to live an ethical, compassionate life.

This is perhaps nowhere more poignantly expressed than in a famous episode from the very end of the Buddha's life. The Buddha was eighty at the time. He had been traveling with his most faithful disciple, Ananda, preaching the *dharma*, and the two of them had reached the small village of Kushinagara. The Buddha had just contracted food poisoning and was growing weak. He realized that the moment of his death was near, and because he had obtained the state of enlightenment, and was thus no longer generating any *karma*, this would be his last life—upon his death, he would obtain the state of *parinirvana*, beyond all future births and deaths.

When Ananda learned of the imminent death of his beloved teacher and companion, he was overcome with grief, and went off to a remote part of the monastery, where he was found weeping, in a state of utter despair. This is a moment of pure pathos. The Buddha, learning of the distress of his dear companion, called him, and said:

> Enough, Ananda, do not grieve, nor weep. Have I not already told you that the nature of things dictates that we must leave those dear to us? How is it possible, Ananda, that whatever has been born, has come into being, is organized and perishable should not perish? That condition is not possible. For a long time, Ananda, have you waited on the Buddha with a kind, devoted, cheerful, single-hearted, unstinted service of body, with a kind, devoted, cheerful, single-hearted, unstinted service of voice, with a kind, devoted, cheerful, single-hearted, unstinted service of mind. You have acquired much merit, Ananda; exert yourself, and soon will you be free from all depravity. . . . It may be, Ananda, that some of you will think, "The word of The Teacher is a thing of the past; we have now no Teacher." But that, Ananda, is not the correct view. The Doctrine and Discipline, Ananda, which I have taught and enjoined upon you is to be your teacher when I am gone. (*Digha Nikaya* 6.29–6.80)

In short, then, after his death, the Buddha's followers are to find guidance in the teachings that he has left. Elsewhere, the Buddha makes this message quite explicit when he upbraids one of his followers for being too attached to the Buddha's physical body, for wishing to be in his actual presence. He says that the body is just a putrid container, an impermanent form, and not worthy of devotion. Rather, if one wishes to "see" the Buddha, one should learn and follow his teachings.

The Buddha, then, explicitly told his followers that they do not need his living presence in the world, because he has left them all they need. They must, he told them, be lights unto themselves. This, however, did not close the issue. Indeed, the Buddha seemed to recognize that his

followers would continue to desire something of his presence on earth. At
one point, considerably before his death, he had instructed his disciples
on how to properly dispose of his body after his death, so as to eliminate
the possibility that his remains would be worshipped and become the objects of attachment. He said that after his cremation his bones should be
gathered into eight portions, and that these portions should be distributed amongst the rulers of India, to be placed at prominent spots—
crossroads, some texts stipulate. There they would continue long after his
passing from the earth to serve as reminders of his teachings and provide
an opportunity for reflection and meditation: "Those who offer there a
garland, or scents, or paint, or make a salutation, or feel serene joy in their
heart, for a long time that will be to their benefit and well being." Although this may work in theory, in practice, the Buddhists seem, immediately upon the Buddha's death, to have regarded these physical remains as
something more than reminders of the absent teacher.

## RELICS AND RELIQUARIES

Relics—bones, and other objects the Buddha used or came into contact with—are thus ambiguous and rather problematic objects in Buddhism. On the one hand, relics have served as reminders of the Buddha's
own human body and of the susceptibility of that body to the basic principle of *anitya*, impermanence. The Buddha, after all, was a human being,
and like all humans was subject to physical decay. On the other hand,
however, relics have from the very beginning been treated as objects of
great value that have the ability to effect a sense of the continued physical presence of the Buddha. Thus, a relic is able to convey an essential
Buddhist message, as at once a visceral reminder of the impermanence of
all things—including the Buddha—and the need to conquer the thirst for
existence. At the same time, however, a relic is also a physical object that
gives rise to deep emotions—and sometimes attachments—that are in
tension with that basic message; indeed, relics are frequently regarded as
the living Buddha himself. By worshipping the relics, then, monks and
laypersons were able to partake of the continued presence of the Buddha.

Importantly, Buddhists do not consider only body parts as relics; garments worn by the Buddha, his begging bowl, artistic images, combs,
toothpicks, to name only a few, are all, in various contexts, considered his
relics. There are, however, traditionally three categories of relics in early

Buddhism: corporeal relics, such as bones and teeth; relics of use, such as the Buddha's begging bowl or robes; and relics of commemoration, such as artistic images. The dominant emphasis in early Buddhist texts is on corporeal relics; this is evident in the *Mahaparinibbana Sutta*, the text that recounts the Buddha's last days, death, and contains the earliest mention of relics. After all the eight portions of the bodily relics have been distributed, a Brahmin by the name of Dona, who has assisted in the cremation of the Buddha and the division of his bones, is left with no relic portion for himself. He is, however, given the pot in which the bones have been kept as a kind of de facto relic—not a bodily relic, but a relic of use or contact. Although it is not explicitly stated in the text, it would seem that this pot is given to Dona as at once a recognition of his service, but also as a mark of his inferior status (because he is a Hindu).

Relics quickly became extremely important objects in early Buddhism. First, they were objects used in ritual practices. Although the Buddha himself quite explicitly stated that he was not to be worshipped while alive, and certainly not after his death, a variety of early Buddhist sources—canonical texts, commentaries, and inscriptions—quite clearly indicate that Buddhists were doing more than simply remembering the qualities of their dead teacher when they beheld his physical remains. Indeed, in many instances, relics are actually discussed as if they were the Buddha himself, as if they were living objects that contained his purity and spiritual force and even something of his physical being.

Ashoka is credited with spreading relics throughout India. Although the legends about his efforts—which typically state that he divided the original bodily relics into 84,000 portions and had them enshrined in 84,000 monuments spread throughout India—are no doubt exaggerations, it seems that he did, indeed, use the relics and the monuments that contained them as very effective tools in gaining converts to the religion. The Buddha himself had instructed his followers to build *stupas* to house the relics.

A *stupa* is essentially a burial mound, a bell-shaped dome that can be anywhere from only a few inches to hundreds of feet in height. In India and Sri Lanka, remains of these huge *stupas* built as early as the end of the first millennium B.C.E., perhaps dating all the way back to Ashoka's reign, have survived. These structures, simple as they were, became the focal points of Buddhist ritual practice, the centers of devotion for both the monks and the laity. Although, initially, they may have been intended to enshrine only the Buddha's corporeal relics, soon Buddhists were placing nonbodily relics within them, and relics associated not just with the Buddha himself, but also with important monks. This, then, was a crucial element in the spread of Buddhism, for it not only gave Buddhist monks and laypersons a physical gathering place, but it also provided a way to memorialize both the great founder—and, in an important sense, to perpetuate his presence on earth—and later charismatic monks. Two of these *stupas*, one at Sanchi (in modern Madhya Pradesh) and one at Amaravati (in modern Andhra Pradesh), became the focal points of large monastic institutions and attracted pilgrims and monks from throughout India and, as time passed, other parts of Asia. These monuments will be discussed at greater length in a later section of this chapter.

## IMAGES OF THE BUDDHA

The very nature of a sculptural image in Buddhism is complex, and the conception and function of images vary not only over the long course of Buddhist history, but also according to the particular ritual, devotional, and decorative context in which any particular image was situated. Images of the Buddha were thought of, in some sense, as substitutes for the absent teacher. In a story with many different versions throughout Buddhist literature, the very first image is said to have been made, with the Buddha's permission, by a king named Prasenajit, who had a stone replica of the Buddha made while the Buddha was away preaching; in some versions of the story, the image actually preaches to the *sangha* in the master's absence. Images then functioned similarly to relics, and indeed are thought of as a class of relics.

The earliest surviving Buddhist sculpture dates to roughly the third century B.C.E., and the images produced contextually functioned as decorations and visual "texts" in monasteries. Significantly, however, the Buddha himself is absent from these very early images. Instead of the Buddha's physical form, early Buddhist artisans employed a range of visual symbols to communicate aspects of the Buddha's teachings and life story: the wheel of *dharma*, denoting his preaching ("turning") his first sermon, and also, with its eight spokes, the eightfold Buddhist path; the Bodhi tree, which represents the place of his enlightenment (under the tree at Bodhgaya) and comes to symbolize the enlightenment experience itself; the throne, symbolizing his status as "ruler" of the religious realm, and also, through its emptiness, his passage into final *nirvana*; the deer, evoking both the place of his first sermon, the Deer Park at Sarnath, and the protective qualities of the *dharma*; the footprint, which denotes both his former physical presence on earth and his temporal absence; the lotus, symbolic of the individual's journey up through the "mud" of existence, to bloom, with the aid of the *dharma*, into pure enlightenment; and the *stupa*, the reliquary in which are contained the Buddha's physical remains, a powerful symbol of both his physical death and his continued presence in the world.

Much of the very early art produced in India is narrative in both form and function, presenting episodes from the Buddha's life and, particularly, scenes from his prior lives. At such sites as Bharhut and Sanchi in modern Madhya Pradesh, Bodhgaya in modern Bihar, and Amaravati in modern Andhra Pradesh, huge *stupas* were erected as part of the large monastic complexes that began to be built at these sites in the third century B.C.E. Elaborate carvings were made on and around these *stupas*, particularly on the railings that encircled the monuments themselves. Many of these were scenes from the Buddha's prior lives, which were also verbally recorded in the *Jataka* and *Avadana* literature. There were representations of prior buddhas; and there were also depictions of key events in the Buddha's life, such as his miraculous conception, his birth, and his departure from the palace in search of enlightenment.

It has typically been assumed that because the earliest Buddhist artistic images did not depict the Buddha, there must have been a doctrinally based prohibition against such depictions. First articulated by the French art historian Alfred Foucher in 1917, this idea—generally referred to as the "aniconic thesis"—has deeply influenced our understanding of early Buddhist art. The basic assumption has been that there must have been a prohibition against representing the Buddha in the early centuries after his death, perhaps because the Buddha had, at the time of his *parinirvana*, passed forever out of existence, and therefore could only be represented by his absence. Recently, however, scholars have begun to rethink this basic assumption, and have argued that perhaps these early sculptures are not reflective of a theological position, but instead frequently represent scenes after the Buddha's death, scenes of worship at prominent places of pilgrimage linked to key events in his life—such as Bodhgaya, Lumbini, Rajagriha—and are thus intended to serve as ritual records and blueprints, visual prompters for correct veneration. What seems clear, at any rate, is that early Buddhists had a complex understanding of both the form and function of representations of the Buddha, and that any attempt to articulate a univocal theory of early Buddhist art is probably misguided, precisely because of the complex interactions of original intent, ritual and aesthetic context, and individual disposition.

Actual images of the historical Buddha began to appear prominently in two regions sometime around the turn of the first millennium of the Common Era: In Mathura, near modern Agra; and in Gandhara, in what is now modern Afghanistan. In Mathura, large standing images of the Buddha were made in red sandstone. The Buddha in these images is depicted as broad shouldered, wearing a robe, and marked by various *lakshanas*, the thirty-two auspicious marks with which he was born, and which are described in several early texts. These included the *ushnisha*, or protuberance atop the head, elongated earlobes, webbed fingers, *dharmacakra* (wheel of *dharma*) on the palms, and so on. In Gandhara, the Buddha was typically depicted in what appears to be a Greek style of representation, wearing a robe that resembles a chlamys, and with distinctly Western facial features, details that may be evidence that an iconographic exchange took place with the Greeks who inhabited the region at the time of Alexander the Great (late fourth century B.C.E.). Many of the Gandharan Buddha images depict him as seated, forming the *dharmacakra mudra*—symbolizing the turning of the wheel of *dharma*—with his hands. In other images, he is presented in a meditational posture, his body withered by the years of extreme asceticism that preceded his enlightenment. These different iconic forms were employed by Buddhist artisans (and their royal, monastic, and lay patrons) both to emphasize the different moments in the Buddha's life story and to convey visually different aspects of the *dharma*.

Although from the moment they appeared in the Buddhist world visual images were intended to narrate aspects of the Buddha's life and teachings, and therefore function on the ground as visual texts to be read, they were also very much intended to be objects of ritual worship. A wide range of texts are available for making and consecrating Buddhist images, from locally produced manuals in the vernacular to pan-Buddhist iconographic manuals. Perhaps the most common form of worship in the Buddhist world is *buddha puja*, literally, "honoring the Buddha." This ritual typically involves making some sort of offering to a Buddha image (or to a relic or a *stupa*)—a flower, a small lamp, food, or even money. Many images, particularly the stelae that were abundantly produced in the medieval Indian milieu—although this is also an iconographic theme on some of the very earliest Buddhist images—actually depict such worship as part of the sculpture, usually along the base of the image, at what would, in a ritual context, be eye-level for the worshipper. The iconography in such cases, then, serves as a kind of visual guide to proper ritual action.

Buddhist iconography is also frequently intended to focus the mind of the worshipper on the Buddha and his teachings, to serve as a visual aid, and to help the practitioner engage in *buddha anusmrti*, or "recollection of the Buddha." This important form of meditation, which is described in several texts from as early as the first century B.C.E., involves contemplating the Buddha's magnificent qualities and internalizing them, very often with the use of an image, either a sculpture or a painting. The iconography of such images, then, serve a mimetic function, in that the meditator is to emulate the iconographically presented Buddha, and in the process create a mental image; in short, the practitioner is to become like the image, and in the process, like the Buddha himself.

## THE POWER AND PRESENCE OF PLACE

Buddhism could never have established itself in India had it not, very early on, been intimately associated with specific sacred places. The places associated with the life of the Buddha took on a special significance, perhaps even during his lifetime. Indeed, in the *Mahaparinibbana Sutta*, he actually tells Ananda that if someone were to die on a pilgrimage to the holy places associated with his life, that person would "be reborn in a realm of heavenly happiness." Initially, there seem to have been four of these sites: Lumbini, the place of Siddhartha's birth; Bodhgaya, where Shakyamuni attained enlightenment and thus became the Buddha; Sarnath, where the newly enlightened Buddha delivered his first sermon; and Kushinagara, where he died. The Buddhist tradition credits Ashoka with marking these sites as particularly significant—he went on a pilgrimage to visit the actual sites, and also built monasteries and monuments there. Indeed, Ashoka is credited with having gone on the first pilgrimage in Buddhist history, the famous *Dharma Yatra*, shortly after his conversion to Buddhism. In the centuries after his reign, a larger set of sacred sites was developed, some of which were also associated with the

Buddha's life, while others gained prominence as monastic centers and places of worship, such as Sanchi and Amaravati.

Although Siddhartha was physically born in Lumbini, it has remained a rather small and minor place of pilgrimage. As the birthplace of the religion, the single most significant place in all of Buddhism is Bodhgaya, so much so that the first-century author Ashvaghosha, in his *Buddhacarita*, calls Bodhgaya "the navel of the universe." It is not certain when Bodhgaya became a place of pilgrimage, but it may be that its significance dates to Ashoka's visit in the third century B.C.E. In some later versions of the Ashoka story, he is said to have gone to Bodhgaya before his conversion to Buddhism and actually cut down the great Bodhi tree, under which the Buddha had attained enlightenment; the tree, however, miraculously grew back overnight. At any rate, after his conversion, he went to Bodhgaya and seems to have erected at least one of his pillars there, and may also have established an early monastic community at the site. In the following centuries, Bodhgaya would become a lively monastic center and a significant pilgrimage place. In addition to the Bodhi tree, pilgrims were drawn to Bodhgaya because of the presence there of the *Vajra Asana*, the seat on which the Buddha was said to have attained enlightenment. According to the accounts of the fourth-century Chinese pilgrim Faxian, there were also various *stupas* scattered about the site, enshrining the relics of significant monks.

There was also a large temple structure at Bodhgaya, called the Mahabodhi Temple, perhaps built as early as the third century B.C.E., although its actual origins are obscure. Certainly, contemporary Buddhist pilgrims from all over the world flock to the temple, and it may be that very early on, the temple was a significant reason for pilgrimage to the site. The current temple—which has been rebuilt several times over the centuries, but is modeled on a much older structure—stands nearly 160 feet high and is some 48 feet square at its base. It houses in its upper stories relics of the Buddha, with various shrines occupying the lower floors. In the central shrine is a large image of the Buddha in the *bhumisparsha* position, the moment when he defeated the evil Mara.

In addition to the Bodhi tree, the *Vajra Asana*, and the Mahabodhi Temple, Bodhgaya has a significant monastic center, known as the Mahabodhi Vihara, housing as many as 1,000 monks, with dozens of buildings—living quarters, lecture halls, study areas, kitchens, and dining halls. The monastery at Bodhgaya was particularly important to monks from Sri Lanka, Thailand, and Burma. Indeed, when the temple and the monastery fell into a state of disrepair in the twelfth century, after Buddhism had all but died out in India, it was the monks who kept the place alive and, eventually, led to its rebirth in the late nineteenth century.

Another very important place of pilgrimage in early Buddhism, and one that also figures prominently in Buddhist sculpture, was Sarnath, near the modern city of Banaras, where the Buddha delivered his first sermon in the Deer Park. Again, Ashoka seems to have visited Sarnath on his *dharma* tour. However, it is really in sculpture that Sarnath rose to prominence, since the scene of the Buddha preaching his first sermon was one of the most common forms of representing him from the very earliest period of Buddhist art. The Buddha is typically seated in such images, forming the *dharmacakra mudra* (denoting his first teaching of the *dharma*), and he is often flanked by several smaller figures—the five monks who first heard the sermon, the laywoman Sujata who offered him the modest gift of food that gave him strength to attain enlightenment, two deer, as well as an image of the wheel.

As Buddhism spread south from the Gangetic plains, several important monastic complexes sprang up, among them the temples at Sanchi and Bharhut. These are some of the earliest and most magnificent of Buddhist structures. Sanchi and Bharhut seem to date to the time of Ashoka—he had an engraved pillar erected at Sanchi, for instance, and may have been responsible for the building of Sanchi's Great *Stupa*. Perhaps most magnificent about these places are the elaborately carved stone railings that encircle the *stupas*, for, on these railings Buddhist artisans carved beautiful scenes from the *Jataka* tales as well as scenes from the Buddha's life. In an important sense, these carvings present a kind of visual narrative of not only the Buddha's life story, but also of Buddhism itself. They also present an important record of Buddhist devotional activity, since, as we have already seen, these images seem to be as much a narrative device as a visual guide to proper ritual.

The Great *Stupa* at Amaravati, the ruins of which are located in what is now the South Indian state of Andhra Pradesh, near the coast of the Bay of Bengal and on the banks of the Krishna River, must have been one of the most spectacular monuments in the Buddhist world, with a large monastic complex connected to it housing hundreds of monks. The main *stupa* was some 140 feet in diameter and 100 feet tall, and may have been built as early as Ashoka's time; indeed, there is an inscription that attributes the structure to Ashoka himself, although this may well be apocryphal. Around the *stupa*'s base were carved hundreds of images, which, like those at Sanchi and Bharhut, presented scenes from the Buddha's life and from the *Jataka* stories.

One of the most important aspects of these great temples—and there were dozens more spread throughout India—was that they were instrumental in the emergence of Buddhism as a pan-Indian religion and essential in its continued vitality throughout the subcontinent. On one level, these temples continued to tell the story of the Buddha and Buddhism in stone. On another, the basic ritual forms expressed at Sanchi, Bharhut, and Amaravati continued for centuries to be replicated throughout the Buddhist world. Furthermore, not only did the artisans and patrons at Amaravati, as well as at Bharhut and Sanchi, establish a basic ritual lexicon, they also established, when they did actually represent the Buddha, the basis of what would become a standard set of significant events in the Buddha's life. Thus, sites such as these, which were never visited by the Buddha, were significant as monastic centers and as devotional gathering places; at the same time, they all were instrumental in preserving the places associated with the life of the Buddha.

Thus, for instance, many of Amaravati's images depict multiple events in the Buddha's life, events linked to specific places. A very elaborate slab from the temple's railings is a good example here. The image depicts an elaborately detailed *stupa* with various scenes from the Buddha's life, including a standing Buddha in the center, displaying the *abhayamudra*, flanked by several much smaller standing and kneeling worshippers; a scene that appears to be the dream of Mahamaya, as well as the birth of Shakyamuni; the Buddha seated in meditation; the Buddha delivering his first sermon; and other scenes of teaching and veneration. What is particularly significant about this image is the arrangement of multiple scenes around a single central image, scenes that, when taken together—as they would have been by the worshipper in the ritual context in which the slab was originally situated—can be seen to present the Buddha's entire life story in condensed form: birth, enlightenment, teaching, and death (as signified by the *stupa* form of the dome itself), plus various paradigmatically significant events.

This image allows the ritual participant to be, in an important sense, a part of these events, not just in his or her mind, but also in time and space—the image, in this sense, makes the events and the people and the places present. And in presenting such scenes together, as part of a single image, the artisans have allowed the worshipper to be a part of the ongoing life of the Buddha and the *dharma*. Thus, although the Buddha himself is absent from the world, he continues to be made present, and thus available, through images and the devotional rituals associated with them. By the second or third century C.E., a standard iconographic form in Buddhism had emerged. Artisans presented the life of the Buddha on a single stone image—usually a single image surrounded by four or six scenes from his life, almost always including, at least, the enlightenment, the first sermon, and the *parinirvana*. Eventually, a standard set of eight scenes was developed, the iconographic form known as the *ashtamahapratiharya*, or "eight great events," presenting not only a visual narrative, as it were, of the significant events in the Buddha's life, but also a kind of map of his life, a place-specific narrative that presented both event and place. These eight scenes all represented actual places that could be, and were, physically visited by Buddhist pilgrims—famously, by the Chinese pilgrims Faxian (in the fifth century C.E.) and Xuanzang (in the eighth), and also by countless other pilgrims over the centuries. The Buddha's life, and in important ways his person as well, were preserved by the artistic images and the pilgrimage places they depicted.

The devotional dynamics of such images—which is also expressed textually, in sometimes very complex philosophical discussion of images and ritual that are contained in the commentaries on the canonical texts— are such that the believing viewer is made *past*. The image transports one into the past, the ideal time when the Buddha was alive, preaching the *dharma*, defeating Mara, and so on; the image transports the viewer into a time when these places were not merely shrines, but locales where the Buddha was present, and the Buddha was not merely a figurative presence, but a living being.

## CONCLUSION

Buddhists responded to the physical absence of their beloved teacher in a variety of ways, then. They continued to study and preach the *dharma* long after he had died, to keep him present, as he himself had said they should, by keeping his teachings alive. But they also kept him present by representing him in stone, by making images of him which were, very often, treated as living beings—they were seen not merely as representations, but as embodiments.

One way early Buddhism articulated the Buddha's continued presence in the world was by formulating a theory of the Buddha's two bodies, or *kayas*. The first body was called the *Rupakaya*, which literally means the "form body." This was the Buddha's physical body when he was alive. After he died—and again, it is important that it was his final death, his *parinirvana*—his form body would be replaced by his *Dharmakaya*, the body of his teachings, a sometimes-complex metaphysical doctrine that seems to be based in the Buddha's admonishment of Ananda just before his death: "Do not become attached to my physical form," he said, "because my real form will continue in my teachings."

Although this understanding of the Buddha's continued presence in the world, despite his physical absence, was an extremely powerful and important element in the ongoing life of Buddhism in India and elsewhere in Asia, an important new school emerged sometime around 100 C.E. that presented a very different understanding of the Buddha's presence in the world, and a very different interpretation of his teachings. That school was called the Mahayana, the Great Vehicle, and it is the subject of the next chapter.

## CHAPTER 5

# THE EMERGENCE
# OF THE MAHAYANA

The first few centuries after the death of the Buddha were a time of constant change in Buddhism. Because the Buddha did not leave a written body of scriptures, as the tradition developed and became established first in India and then in other parts of Asia, the process of the formation of a canon—a standard set of the Buddha's teachings—was sometimes fractious. His immediate disciples had transmitted his teachings to one another, preserving them orally, and when his followers met to attempt to establish what he had actually said, what was *buddhavacana* (the Buddha's own speech), disagreements arose. There were also philosophical debates about what some of his teachings meant. Furthermore, because the Buddha did not leave a specific set of acceptable ritual practices, debates inevitably arose as to what was and was not appropriate devotional behavior. Finally, there was the often-contentious issue of monastic discipline, or *vinaya*.

On one level, this fluidity might be seen to be a negative element in the developing tradition, since it sometimes led to serious schisms. On the other, though, it was precisely this openness to debate and discussion that helped Buddhism become established in India: because the Buddha had insisted that one's personal progress on the Path was up to one's own effort, very little in the religion could be taken as simply given. This, then, would have allowed the individual monk or layperson a great deal of religious freedom, and this may well have been attractive, standing as it does in such stark contrast to the strictures of the Brahmanical religion of the period. That said, however, there were often serious schisms and divisions within Buddhism, the most serious and long lasting of which was the emergence of a new school sometime around the first century C.E. This new school called itself the Mahayana, the Great Vehicle.

## SCHISM AND DEBATE

It would be wrong, certainly, to think—as many scholars of Buddhism have—of the emergence of the Mahayana in the first century as some sort of doctrinal bomb that was suddenly dropped on the Buddhist world. Equally misleading is the other standard view of the rise of the Mahayana: that it was the result of lay Buddhists' desires to make the Path more open to them and less oriented to the monk. In fact, the school that eventually became known as the Mahayana did not, initially, see itself as a school at all. Rather, it was most probably a relatively small group of monks who were trying to work out the meaning of the Buddha's teachings and found themselves at odds with some of the prevailing ideas of the time. Furthermore, it is important to state at the outset that the monks who identified with the emerging Mahayana did not see themselves as revolutionary iconoclasts. Indeed, we know that these monks continued to live in monasteries with other, non-Mahayana monks; in other words, their ideas were not simply critiques of existing doctrines and practices, but were also different interpretations, in keeping with the very spirit of Buddhism.

The Buddhist chronicles, as well as various inscriptions, provide evidence of the councils that were held in order to resolve some of these issues, as well as to come to some sort of doctrinal agreement. The first of these councils was held very soon after the death of the Buddha, during the rains retreat at Rajagriha, and seems to have been, a gathering of the Buddha's immediate followers to attempt to record, orally, exactly what he had taught. A few sources record a second, smaller, gathering the following year, although whether this was a different council or an extension of the first is unclear. The second major council, as we have seen, was held in the city of Vaishali, sometime in the fourth century B.C.E., and centered on issues of monastic discipline, not doctrine, although doctrinal issues were no doubt indirectly involved. Sometime shortly after the council at Vaishali, however, a series of schisms arose in the Buddhist communities, disagreements over doctrinal issues.

Thus, by about the third century B.C.E., the Buddha's disciples had divided themselves into what Buddhist historical sources describe as at least eighteen different schools (perhaps more), each associated, roughly, with a particular region. There were the Mahasamghikas in and around Pataliputra; the Sarvastivadins in Kashmir and Gandhara; the Caitikas in

Andhra; the Lokuttaravadins in Madhya Pradesh, and so on. Mostly, these were not in fact separate schools so much as groups of monks who held different opinions on relatively minor points—monastic discipline issues, as we have seen, and also philosophical interpretations of the Buddha's teachings. As this process of more and more detailed and complex understandings of the Buddha's message progressed, some serious issues led to increasingly serious divisions within the *sangha*. We have already seen that early Buddhists spent a great deal of time dissecting reality and the concepts that are used to understand reality; indeed, this is at the very heart of the *Abhidharma*, the huge canonical body of doctrinal interpretation and philosophical speculation. One such issue revolved around the status of the *arhats*, those monks who had followed the Buddha's teachings to the point of enlightenment.

For instance, there arose the question as to whether an *arhat* could, once enlightened, slip out of that state. One group of monks, the Mahasamghikas, were quite critical of the *arhat*, and saw him as a lesser being, capable of falling out of enlightenment. In contrast, they pointed to the Buddha, whose enlightenment was absolute. They were also highly critical of what they called the *shravakas*, or "hearers," a label that may have been intended to portray their monastic rivals as mere passive receivers of the teachings. But at the heart of the debate was the question whether or not the Buddha continued to be an active force in the world. The Mahasamghikas tended to argue that he was. The other main group that emerged during this period, the Sarvastivadins, tended to see the Buddha as present in the form of his teachings, but not as an active force. They would, eventually, see their opponents' view as a logical impossibility, and occasionally charge them with what was, essentially, a heretical doctrinal position.

At any rate, the Mahasamghikas offered up a rather bold interpretation of the whole issue of the person and presence of the Buddha, an interpretation that grew into the very heart of the Mahayana's teachings—the doctrine of the bodhisattva.

## THE BODHISATTVA: A NEW MODEL OF THE IDEAL BEING

At the very core of the emergent Mahayana school is the concept of the bodhisattvas. They are the enlightened beings who, unlike the *arhats*, choose not to pass out of existence upon their physical death, but continue to be active presence in the world, coming to the aid of those beings still trapped in *samsara*. It is difficult to pinpoint when exactly this idea emerged in Buddhist circles, but it is clear that it is an idea that emerged out of the sometimes-contentious discussions about the nature of the Buddha and his continued presence in the world.

As briefly discussed in Chapter 4, this is first articulated in the context of the doctrine of the various bodies, or *kayas*, of the Buddha, a doctrine that seems to predate the actual emergence of the Mahayana. The first of these bodies—which are not in fact conceived of strictly as physical forms, but rather more like the different ways in which the Buddha continues to be present in the world—is the *Dharmakaya*. This is the Buddha's form as wisdom, truth, and the real nature of reality. This is that which characterizes the Buddha as the Buddha, and it was later actually called "Buddhaness" by Mahayana thinkers. As such, then, the *Dharmakaya* is not strictly limited to the teachings left by the Buddha— although it has them as its essence—but is understood to be the whole collection of wonderful qualities that are known as "the Buddha." This form of the Buddha necessarily continues after his death. The second body is called the *Rupakaya*, or "form body" (also referred to as the *Nirmanakaya*, or transformation body). This is the earthly form, or manifestation, of the Buddha. Later Mahayana theologians added to these two a third body, a more rarefied form called the *Sambhogakaya*, or "enjoyment body," which is the form of the Buddha that those who have attained enlightenment "enjoy" and interact with.

Related to this idea of multiple bodies of the Buddha was the emergence of the concept of the bodhisattva, what is perhaps the hallmark of the Mahayana schools. Although a common word in the earliest of Buddhist texts, the earlier Buddhist schools held that once the Buddha had attained enlightenment, he taught the *dharma* to his disciples and then, on his death, attained final *nirvana*, thus ending his existence in the realm of *samsara* forever. The Buddha's immediate disciples, the *arhats*, who likewise mastered his teachings after his death, and like the Buddha, upon attaining enlightenment entered *nirvana* after death. Perhaps most radical about the Mahayana monks' new doctrinal interpretations was that this ideal, the *arhat*, was, they argued, actually a contradiction of one of the most basic elements of the Buddha's teachings—compassion. The Mahayanists derisively labeled the *arhats Pratyekabuddhas*, or "solitary

Buddhas," and posited that the Buddha and all other truly enlightened beings "postponed" final *nirvana* out of their compassion for the sufferings of other beings, choosing to remain in *samsara* to perfect their own Buddhahood and work for the benefit of all other beings, until each one attains enlightenment.

There are a number of important elements to be noted here. For one thing, all beings were conceived by the Mahayana as at once having the innate potential to become a buddha, and also sharing a kind of universal enlightenment as well. The Path, then, was reconceived as being the path of the bodhisattva, a path that takes many, many lives, but is intent on developing *bodhicitta*, the quality of the awakened mind, and thus the very quality of enlightenment, a quality that fundamentally shifts one's attention away from the self to a selfless concern for the well-being of others. Each bodhisattva takes a vow to help other beings, and continues to do so indefinitely, a vow that involves cultivating a list of six (later expanded to ten) perfections, or *paramitas*. These are:

1. Generosity (*dana*)

2. Morality (*shila*)

3. Patience and forbearance (*kshanti*)

4. Vigor, the endless and boundless energy that they employ in their helping of others (*virya*)

5. Meditation (*dhyana*)

6. Wisdom (*prajna*)

7. Skillful means (*upaya*)

8. Conviction (*pranidhana*)

9. Strength (*bala*)

10. Knowledge (*jnana*)

With the rise of the ideal of the bodhisattva came also the development of a complex pantheon of enlightened beings who figured prominently in the iconography of the emergent school. Indeed, with the rise of the Mahayana there was a kind of iconographic explosion in India, accompanied by the development of numerous new sculptural forms and devotional rituals.

Three of the most popular and most important bodhisattvas in the early Mahayana were Manjushri, Avalokiteshvara, and Maitreya.

*Manjushri*—Especially associated with wisdom, Manjushri is a key figure in numerous early Mahayana scriptures, and he has been the focus of significant devotional activity throughout the Mahayana world. His name literally means "gentle glory." In sculptures, he is typically depicted as a handsome young man holding aloft a sword—the incisive sword of wisdom with which he cuts through delusion and ignorance—in one hand and a lotus in the other. A consistent element in his iconography is the representation of a book—sometimes he holds the text aloft, sometimes it rises out of a lotus to one of his sides—which is described in the iconographic manuals that were often used by Buddhist artisans and also by worshippers as the *Perfection of Wisdom* text, of which he is the manifestation.

*Avalokiteshvara*—He is the quintessential Buddhist savior figure, and the embodiment of compassion, perhaps the most popular of all bodhisattvas in India. His name is indicative of his character: it means "the lord who sees all," in the sense that he sees the suffering of all living beings and responds immediately. He saves his followers from a set of dangers that are metaphors for the perils inherent in the world of *samsara*: fire, drowning in a river, being lost at sea, murder, demonic attack, fierce beasts and noxious snakes or insects, legal punishment, attack by bandits, falling from precipices, extremes of weather, internecine civil or military unrest, and others. In the sculpture of the early Mahayana in India, he is depicted in dozens of forms: frequently, he has several eyes, denoting his compassionate omniscience, and sometimes multiple heads, as in the *dasamukha* (ten-faced) iconography; he also nearly always has multiple hands, in which he holds various implements that aid him in his salvific endeavors.

*Maitreya*—The Buddha of the future, the final manifestation of Buddhaness to appear in the world. According to some Mahayana scriptures, building on an idea mentioned in the early Pali texts, eventually the Buddha's teachings will lose their potency due to the natural decay of the world. When things become unbearable and no spiritual progress is possible, Maitreya will be reborn, who will provide for the welfare of all beings and promote a new set of teachings. In sculpture, he is often depicted as a crowned, royal figure (often with a Buddha image or *stupa* on his forehead), and he frequently displays the *dharmachakra mudra*, the gesture of religious discourse, since it is he who will deliver the final version of the *dharma* that will release all beings from *samsara*.

A range of divine and semidivine female figures, who function very similarly to the male bodhisattvas, are also discussed and described in Mahayana texts. It has been suggested that the existence of these female figures in the Mahayana pantheon is indicative of a more gender-inclusive attitude in Mahayana Buddhism. This is certainly possible, although it is not always clear from the texts. What can be said for certain is that in Mahayana symbolism and rhetoric, there is an elevation of female imagery and metaphor. Two of the most popular female figures are Tara and Prajnaparamita.

Tara emerges in the Mahayana as a divine savior who protects and nurtures her devotees; her name literally means "star," and she was perhaps originally associated, in particular, with guiding sailors, and is sometimes referred to as *jagat tarini*, the "deliverer of the world." She is depicted in numerous forms, sometimes seated with a book, sometimes standing displaying variations of the *abhayamudra* (the gesture of no fear) or making a hand gesture of giving, and is intimately associated with the lotus, denoting her characteristic purity.

Prajnaparamita is the personification of the *Perfection of Wisdom* texts (*Prajnaparamita Sutras*), and is described as wisdom incarnate, the divine "mother" of all enlightened beings. She is typically seated, legs crossed, and has either two or four arms; she almost always forms the *dharmacakra mudra*, holding both a lotus (emblematic of the purity of her teachings) and the text of which she is the embodiment.

In addition to the bodhisattvas and the female divinities, the Mahayana also propounded, extending their understanding of the continued presence of the Buddha in the world, the concept that there were both multiple buddhas and also multiple plains of existence. This can become very complex. Essentially, they took the idea, which, as we have seen, appears very early in Buddhism, that the Buddha remains, in some sense, an active presence in the world, and simply expanded this. It is not just that the Buddha himself remains present; rather, his essential nature, his *buddhata* (literally, Buddhaness), remains, not only in the form of the bodhisattvas, but also in the form of other buddhas. These buddhas, who are at least theoretically infinite in number, reside in various higher realms, called Pure Lands.

## LEGITIMIZING "NEW" SCRIPTURES AND DOCTRINES

One issue that immediately arises with the Mahayana is, if what the Mahayana presents really is true doctrine, then why did the Buddha himself not speak about such matters? Why did he make no mention of these bodhisattvas? Indeed, the non-Mahayana monks, those who called themselves initially Sthaviravadins and later became known as the Theravadins, charged that the Mahayana was simply inventing new doctrines and new scriptures. As such, their ideas were at best misinterpretations and at worst heresy, because they did not meet the basic criterion for doctrinal legitimacy—they were not *buddhavacana*.

This was not a new problem in Buddhism. According to some early scriptures, as well as the Theravadin historical chronicles, the Buddhist Canon was set at the first council, held at Rajagriha shortly after the Buddha's death. The Theravadins claimed that they strictly adhered to this canon—hence their name, the "doctrine of the elders." In fact, though, there was much ongoing debate over the issue of what should or should not be considered "doctrine" in the centuries after the Buddha's death. Several different versions of the canon seem to have been in circulation, as well as different versions of the *Jataka* and *Avadana*—stories about the Buddha's prior lives and his activities in his final manifestation on earth. The Sarvastivadins, for example, are known to have complained that there were monks who had added new—and false—*Vinaya* and *Abhidharma* texts to the canon. As the movement that eventually became known as the Mahayana grew, these complaints became more and more pointed. The Theravadins frequently charged that the monks of the Mahayana simply invented new scriptures, *sutras* that were not the speech of the Buddha but the invention of poets.

Although it is dubious on purely historical evidence, the Mahayana in fact presents a corpus of "new" *sutras* that it claims were spoken by Shakyamuni himself. There are different versions of how this might have been possible: One, for instance, has it that the Buddha originally taught the Mahayana doctrines but that eventually there were no competent teachers or students left to carry on the teachings, so he had them entrusted to his friends the Nagas—the mythical serpents of many Buddhist texts who protect the religion—until a skillful teacher emerged (often said to be the great South Indian philosopher Nagarjuna).

At any rate, even though it seems fairly certain that these *sutras* were not the actual speech of the Buddha, it is equally certain that the monks of the Mahayana genuinely saw themselves as propounders of a doctrine that was more in keeping with the teachings of the Buddha than that offered up by their Theravada counterparts. Although it would be impossible to cover all of the significant points of Mahayana doctrine in this context, some of the most important ideas of this new school were the following:

*Emptiness, or shunyata.* A concept that first appears in the *Perfection of Wisdom* texts, this idea extends the Buddha's teachings about dependent origination, and posits that since all phenomena are dependent for their being on some other thing, they cannot be considered, in themselves, to have any essence or ultimate reality. The first-century thinker Nagarjuna introduces the most radical understanding of this concept, arguing that just as the terms "long" and "short" take on meaning only in relation to each other and are themselves devoid of independent qualities (longness or shortness), so too do all phenomena (all *dharmas*) lack own being (*svabhava*). If a thing were to have an independent and unchanging own being, Nagarjuna reasons, then it would follow that it is neither produced nor existent, because origination and existence presuppose change and transience. All things, physical as well as mental, can originate and develop only when they are empty of own being. Nevertheless, Nagarjuna contends, elements do have what he calls a conventional reality, so that we still interact with them, think thoughts, and so on, even if ultimately they are empty of reality. Related to this is the concept of skillful means, *upaya*, which refers to the bodhisattva's employment of whatever means necessary to help beings move toward enlightenment. Language, for instance, is itself empty, in that it depends on external references to make sense, but language is necessary in order to spread the *dharma*.

*Wisdom.* In the Pali texts of the Theravada, wisdom, or *panna*, is described as being the penultimate step on the Buddhist path; it is wisdom that leads, essentially, directly to enlightenment. For the Mahayana monks, this wisdom—*prajna* in Sanskrit, in which they composed their *sutras*—became paramount, the focus of their understanding of the Buddha's *dharma*. Indeed, perhaps the earliest texts that can be said to be purely Mahayana were the *Perfection of Wisdom* (*Prajnaparamita*) *Sutras*, which range in length from only a few dozen verses to 100,000. Wisdom is not to be confused with knowledge, but is a radically different way of perceiving and responding to the world. It is that wisdom that enables one to see through illusion, which cuts through grasping and the suffering it engenders, and that leads to enlightenment. The bodhisattvas are, according to the Mahayana, those beings who have perfect *prajna*.

*Compassion.* The Mahayana texts place a great deal of emphasis on the selfless compassion of the buddhas and the bodhisattvas. It is, for instance, Avalokiteshvara's perfectly realized compassion that causes him to come to the aid of suffering beings. Again, this is not a new idea, but rather one that the Mahayana monks felt was overlooked or underemphasized by their Theravada counterparts. The Buddha himself, some texts argue, attained enlightenment out of his own compassion for the suffering in the world—recall that he says, explicitly, that he is abandoning his life as a prince and father not out of selfishness, but out of compassion. He sets out not to save himself, but to save the world. Thus for the Mahayana, this compassion is at the root of the Buddha's message. It is this compassion, furthermore, that enables the bodhisattva and leads him or her to stay in the world to assist other living beings who are still floundering in the sea of *samsara*.

*Skillful Means.* The idea that the buddhas and bodhisattvas are able to help beings using any means necessary, and that they do so with the enlightened knowledge of what each being most needs and is most able to comprehend, is integral to Mahayana thought; this is skillful means, or *upaya*. A classic example of this is found in a later story, "The Parable of the Burning House." The bodhisattva Avalokiteshvara sees several children trapped in a burning house, and rather than yell "Fire, Fire," which he sees will only frighten them, he tells them that he has wonderful toys for them to play with outside of the house, and they run out, saved. In other words, the bodhisattva tailors the dharmic message to the particular pupil.

*The Doctrine of the Two Truths.* Related to the idea of skillful means, this is a sometimes-complex philosophical doctrine, most famously propounded by Nagarjuna, which holds, essentially, that there is an ultimate and a relative reality. The ultimate reality is that all things are empty, and thus unreal, only illusions created by ignorance. The relative reality, however, is our perception of them. Words, for instance, are ultimately empty, and are dependent on something else for their meaning; however, words are necessary, in a relative sense, in order to make the ultimate reality known.

It should be clear that these doctrines really are not new. Indeed, the Mahayana monks did not see themselves as presenting something new at all, but felt that they were, essentially, returning to the real heart of the Buddha's message, a message that they felt some monks—most notably those concerned with the philosophical complexity of the Abhidharma— had lost the essence of. Ironically, perhaps, as the Mahayana expanded in India and eventually spread to other parts of Asia, especially China and Japan, it too became more and more philosophically complex, and thus in a sense was guilty of the very philosophical excess that it was, originally, attempting to correct.

## CONCLUSION

In a sense, it would seem that the new Mahayana and the older Theravada schools would have seen each other as adversaries, and in some important ways this was indeed the case. Each school polemically attacked the other, charging them with propounding heretical doctrines and practices. However, this is only part of the picture. First, it was only later that the two schools really became distinctly defined. Initially, as we have seen, they were simply different subsects of a single Buddhism, groups of monks with different interpretations of the Buddha's message. Second, it is clear from inscriptional evidence that monks who identified themselves as Theravadins (or Sthaviravadins) and those who identified themselves as Mahayanists (or Mahasamghikas) lived in the same monasteries. This implies, then, that they saw themselves not as enemies, but as coreligionists, each pursuing the same goal along slightly different, but ultimately parallel, paths.

This is in keeping with the fundamental spirit of Buddhism, in that the Buddha recognized, quite explicitly, that there were necessarily different ways to progress toward enlightenment and that different people had different abilities to comprehend and follow his teachings. It may be that the Mahayana was successful in India and elsewhere precisely because it appealed to a different group of people than those who were drawn to the Theravada. Unfortunately, the historical evidence to really demonstrate this point is rather sketchy. What can be said with certainty, however, is that the emergence of the Mahayana is best understood in the context of a constantly changing Buddhism. From the moment it emerged in India, Buddhism adapted to a variety of contexts, and as it adapted, it necessarily changed. But as the Buddha so consistently emphasized, change is the very nature of the world.

## CHAPTER 6

# CONCLUSION: THE DECLINE OF BUDDHISM IN INDIA AND ITS RISE ELSEWHERE

Buddhism has always been a missionizing religion. As we have seen, as Buddhism became more established in its homeland, India, it also spread to other parts of Asia: Sri Lanka to the south; Burma, Thailand, and Cambodia to the southeast; China and Japan to the east; Nepal and Tibet to the north. As it did so, Buddhism changed in significant ways, adapting to its various local contexts. New philosophical ideas, new ritual practices, and new art forms were developed. Thus, in China, Taoist and Confucianist ideas were incorporated into Buddhism, and in Tibet the indigenous Bon tradition became an integral part of Tibetan Buddhism. Buddhism also eventually made its way to the West, where it underwent even more dramatic changes.

Ironically, as Buddhism expanded outside of its homeland, it also began to decline there. In this final chapter, we will explore some of the reasons for the gradual disappearance of Buddhism in its homeland, and then turn to a discussion of how Buddhism has continued to flourish outside of India, particularly in the West.

## WHY BUDDHISM DIED OUT IN INDIA

As various Mahayana Buddhist schools developed in India after the first few centuries of the Common Era, the Buddhist pantheon expanded tremendously, especially with the introduction of the various bodhisattvas. It has been generally assumed that the bodhisattvas were one of the reasons Buddhism continued to thrive in India during this period. They offered the Buddhist layperson an image of compassion, a comforting aid in the long journey toward enlightenment. Although it may be true that the Mahayana image of the bodhisattva helped Buddhism gain a degree of popular support, it is probably an oversimplification. For at the same time, Buddhism had become an increasingly philosophical affair in India, and as monks became more concerned with scholastic issues—incredibly complex philosophical issues, the abstruse minutiae of logic—they also became increasingly removed from the life of the layperson.

Beginning in the fifth and sixth centuries, huge monasteries began to be built in India, some of them housing upward of 10,000 monks, monasteries that were very much like modern universities in the West. It would be inaccurate to suggest that all Buddhist monks in medieval India were scholastically oriented, or even that they were actively engaged in philosophical speculation such as that found in the large *Abhidharma* compendiums or the voluminous Mahayana doctrinal examinations. Many monks continued to live very much as the Buddha himself proscribed, as simple, itinerant ascetics who interacted with laypeople largely on a local level as they passed through their villages, or resided on a semipermanent basis in small village temples and monasteries. However, the monasteries of northeastern India were the heart of Buddhism as an institution—even if there was no centralized institutional control, ever, in Indian Buddhism—and as such they tended to be quite uninvolved with lay matters.

This has several important practical ramifications. Because the laity was not intimately involved in scholastic matters, they tended to direct their *dana* activities to local monks outside of the context of the large monastic universities. In order to survive, therefore, these monastic universities had to seek material support elsewhere, and they found it where monks had traditionally found such support: with the king.

Buddhist kings had long been prominent in the various kingdoms of northern India, beginning with the Kushana dynasty in the early centuries of the first millennium and extending to the Palas, a lineage of kings who ruled much of northern India beginning in the eighth century. By the tenth or eleventh century, though, this support was beginning to wane, and the Pala kings began to shift their royal patronage to Hinduism, particularly Vaishnava Hinduism.

This is not the place to delve into the complexities of Vaishnava Hinduism. However, there are several aspects of this form of Hinduism that may have made it particularly attractive to Indian kings. First, there is the simple fact that devotional Hinduism was on the rise. This may have been due, in part, to the fact that Vaishnava devotionalism significantly downplayed caste, and was thus open to all Hindus. Salvation was, at least theoretically, thus not a matter of birth or the ability to perform particular rituals in a particular way—rituals that were largely the province of the high-caste brahmins—but a matter of individual devotion and piety.

Perhaps more importantly, because devotional Hinduism downplayed the significance of caste, kings and other political figures may have found it especially attractive. In other words, they may have seen an opportunity for religious status—which was closely tied to political legitimacy in India—in much the same way that kings in the sixth century B.C.E. had found Buddhism to be an attractive religious affiliation. But in the case of Vaishnava Hinduism, there was an added element to this openness: in the root text of the Vaishnava movement within Hinduism, the *Bhagavadgita* (as well as in the larger *Mahabharata* of which it is a part), the heroes are kings, and thus *kshatriyas*. The god Krishna, an *avatara* (literally, "descent") of the great god Vishnu, comes to the aid of the kings and helps them restore *dharma*, or order, in the world. Indeed, these texts elevate the status of the king in the religion by making an explicit link between the king's duty to maintain social order and religious progress, and the model king is, in this context, thought to be one who acts as Vishnu himself does—protecting *dharma*. During this period, not surprisingly, Vishnu is typically depicted in Hindu sculpture as a ruler, with a crown and other royal regalia.

As Indian rulers increasingly patronized Hinduism, it became more and more difficult to maintain and administer the large Buddhist monasteries, in part because there simply were not sufficient funds and materials to do so. Indeed, Buddhism may have died out in India—which it did sometime around the end of the twelfth century—largely because it had become too large to sustain itself.

Although the rise of Vaishnava Hinduism and the concomitant wavering royal support for monastic Buddhism clearly had a tremendous impact on the religion's ability to survive and thrive in its homeland, this was not the only factor in Buddhism's demise in India. Indeed, there were powerful internal factors that seem to have contributed to the gradual erosion of Buddhism in India. For, although Buddhist monasticism had indeed become a highly scholastic, highly philosophical endeavor, not all Buddhist monks found this to be the proper religious path. In addition to the simple village monks just mentioned, some monks also began, probably as early as the eighth century, to be highly critical of the scholastic character of Buddhism, and often unleashed powerful rhetorical attacks on their scholastic brethren.

What is more, some of these monks took an alternate route to enlightenment, abandoning the monastery altogether and taking up residence in the forests and jungles to live as solitary seekers. Some of these monks became known as Siddhas, the "masters," or "powerful ones." Initially, the Siddhas were probably solitary individuals, dissenting monks who set off on their own spiritual journeys. But just as the Buddha's earliest followers eventually banded together to form communities of monks, so too did the Siddhas, establishing a large body of philosophical principles and, especially, ritual practices that collectively became, eventually, a new subschool of Buddhism—the Vajrayana, or the Diamond Vehicle, more popularly known as Tantra.

These monks emphasized the fundamental transformative effects of meditation, taking the notion of the bodhisattvas' special powers several steps further than their more mainstream Mahayana counterparts. Through very elaborate meditational and ritual practices, the Siddhas felt that they could transform themselves, not just mentally, but physically as well. Through deep meditation and ritual interaction with specific buddhas and bodhisattvas—practices that included ritual offerings, chanting of powerful verbal formulas (*mantras*), hand gestures (*mudras*), symbolic sexual practices, and visualizations (*sadhanas*)—these monks felt that they could effect a quicker pathway to enlightenment.

It is important to recognize that these monks and their practices were never what could be called "popular religion" in India (although as their teachings and practices spread to Tibet, they became very popular indeed, to the point that the Vajrayana became, and remains to this day, the dominant school of Buddhism there). This is in part due to the simple fact that the Siddhas' teachings and practices were highly esoteric in nature. A monk had to go through a long and arduous initiation process in order to be accepted into the Siddhas' religious world. Furthermore, the Siddhas were intentionally iconoclastic, trying to shock the more mainstream monks out of what Siddhas viewed as their scholastic complacency and their reliance on pure logic for enlightenment. It is not so much the case, then, that the Siddhas drew laypeople away from the larger monastic institutions in India; rather, they introduced a significant degree of dissent within a monastic community that was already in a growing state of crisis. Furthermore, because Hinduism also developed a Tantric tradition alongside that of Buddhism, with a great deal of ritual and philosophical overlapping, it may be that the lines separating the two traditions became increasingly blurred, which may have resulted in further decreased lay and royal support for Buddhist monks and monasteries.

In the final analysis, though, it is impossible to say exactly how and why Buddhism died out in India. There was no single cause, but a complex confluence of forces from both within the monastic communities and outside. At any rate, by the end of the twelfth century, Buddhism was essentially dead in India. But, as it was dying in the country of its emergence, it was thriving elsewhere—in Nepal and Tibet, in China and Japan, in Sri Lanka, and throughout Southeast Asia. Significantly, beginning in the second half of the twentieth century, Buddhism began to make a modest comeback in India, in large part because the social relevance of the Buddha's message was seen as a powerful liberating force for outcasts of India's population. Thus, shortly after India's independence from Britain, B. R. Ambedkar, the chairman of India's Constitutional Committee—often called the father of the Indian Constitution—himself an untouchable, publicly converted to Buddhism, along with thousands of other untouchables, beginning a movement that would eventually grow to some six million converts.

Furthermore, monks from outside of India—from Sri Lanka and Tibet, mostly, but also from Europe and America—began to establish new monastic institutions in and around Bodhgaya, where the Buddha had attained enlightenment. Additionally, with his exile from Tibet in the 1950s, the Dalai Lama, the spiritual and political leader of Tibet's Buddhist population, set up residence in western India, and was there joined by thousands of Tibetan Buddhists, who found in Buddhism's homeland a new religious freedom. Thus, it may be that just as Buddhism emerged in a world of religious and social flux in India precisely because the Buddha offered a compelling spiritual message for such a context, it may well reemerge for the same reason.

## BUDDHISM IN THE WEST

Buddhism first entered the Western consciousness with colonialism. In the nineteenth century, particularly, intellectual interest in Buddhism developed in Europe and North America, leading to the creation of a distinct scholarly field focused on the translation of Buddhist texts from their original languages, as well as their philosophical analysis. Thus, initially at least, Western interest in Buddhism seems to have been largely an academic affair. However, an offshoot of this interest was the gradual availability of books on Buddhist beliefs and practices for the general public. As these ideas became increasingly available, many Europeans and Americans began to turn to Buddhism. Although there have never been huge numbers of Buddhists in the West—estimates vary, but probably no more than 5 million of the world's 500 million Buddhists live in the West—they have been an important religious presence. It is worth asking, though, what it has been that Westerners have found so appealing about Buddhism.

Let us begin with a simple example, that of the Theosophical Society's adoption of Buddhist ideas. The Theosophical Society was founded in 1875 by Henry Steele Olcott, an American lawyer and Civil War colonel, and Helena Petrovna Blavatsky, a Russian émigré who claimed ties to the Russian aristocracy. The Theosophical Society was initially involved with a kind of generalized Eastern spirituality, and especially the occult— Blavatsky put herself forward as a psychic, able to perform physical and mental psychic feats, including levitation and telepathy. Olcott and Blavatsky became increasingly associated with Buddhism, and the two moved to India in the 1880s, Olcott eventually playing a leading role in the Buddhist revival in Sri Lanka at the end of the nineteenth century. Although Olcott was not a scholar, his short summary of Buddhism, *The Buddhist Catechism*, first published in 1881, was widely read in America and England. In this short text, Olcott presents a portrait of Buddhism as a highly rational philosophy, devoid of ritual and superstition.

Olcott's work was hardly the only such account of Buddhism to present such a view of Buddhism to the West; nor was it the most popular. Sir Edwin Arnold, a schoolteacher-turned-poet and journalist, produced a rapturous account of the life of the Buddha, *The Light of Asia*, which became one of the most popular books in Victorian England. It was first published in 1871 and went through over one hundred printings; at the time it was published, it sold about as many copies as Mark Twain's *Huckleberry Finn* and was translated into numerous languages. Although Arnold's book was hardly greeted with unanimous approval in the West—it was denounced, for instance, as "mischievous" and "shallow," and attacked as an affront to Christianity—*The Light of Asia* fed a growing interest in things Asian both in England and in America. What Western audiences seemed to have found so appealing about the book was the combination of, on one hand, the sheer exoticism of India, and on the other the rational portrait of the Buddha and Buddhism. Over the next few decades, dozens of such books were published in the West.

Thus, in the last part of the nineteenth century, Buddhism was championed by many in England, Europe, and America as a highly rational religion rivaling—and for many, surpassing—Protestant Christianity. The Buddha was frequently held up as something like an ideal Victorian gentleman, a great reformer compared to Martin Luther, a man who fought for the abolition of caste and who railed against a corrupt priesthood. Leaving aside the accuracy of such a portrait, it was certainly attractive to many Westerners who found fault in their own religious traditions. This particular image of Buddhism was not the only one that found purchase in the West. Beginning in the early part of the twentieth century, Zen Buddhism in particular became an object of fascination in the West and continues to be a significant presence on the Western religious landscape. Indeed, one need only enter a bookstore in any mall in America to see the presence of Zen: one is confronted almost immediately with a mind-boggling array of "Zen and the Art of" books, topics ranging from fixing motorcycles to changing diapers.

Zen Buddhism has its roots in China. Buddhism entered China probably in the first century C.E., via the Silk Route. In China, certain Buddhist schools put particular emphasis on meditation, and became known as "Ch'an," a transliteration of the Sanskrit word *dhyana*, which means "meditation." They also were no doubt influenced by indigenous Taoist notions of the essential harmony of the natural world. This, however, was only one aspect of Chinese Buddhist thought and practice. As Buddhism developed in Japan, Ch'an Buddhist ideas also took hold—known as Zen, the transliteration into Japanese of the word *dhyana*—but again, this was only one strain of Japanese Buddhist thought and practice.

So, how is it that Zen has become such a prominent presence in Western culture? In part, this has to do with how it was brought to the West in the first place. In contrast to the earlier introduction of Buddhism to the West by Westerners, Zen made its way into Western consciousness via the efforts of an elite group of Japanese intellectuals. Beginning in the last part of the nineteenth century, these Zen Buddhists—most notably the Japanese scholar D. T. Suzuki, who, not insignificantly, himself eventually married a Theosophist—have offered the West a sanitized and decontextualized form of Buddhism, what might even be called a kind of "virtual" Buddhism.

Suzuki, for his part, first came to America in 1897, where he worked with Paul Carus, editor of the journal the *Open Court*, in LaSalle, Illinois. Carus's journal sought to promote the conjoining of science and religion and, more particularly, advocated a kind of universal monism common to all religions. For Carus, Buddhism was the closest of the world's religions to live up to this model, and Suzuki seems to have been particularly influenced by Carus in his conception and presentation of Zen for a Western audience. Suzuki's books—most notably his *An Introduction to Zen Buddhism*, which includes a thirty-page commentary by the psychoanalyst Carl Jung—emphasize the transcendent and mystical nature of Zen. Suzuki, in repackaging Zen for a Western audience, attempted to extract what he saw as the essence of Zen from the larger, culturally embedded practice of Zen Buddhism.

In so doing, Suzuki and his followers put particular emphasis on *satori* (awakening) as the goal of the Zen Buddhist, which was touted as a sudden enlightenment experience that could happen at any time, even in the midst of everyday life, and transform mundane experience into something profoundly spiritual. Certainly, *satori* is an important element in Zen Buddhist teachings, but many scholars have seen Suzuki's portrayal of Zen spirituality as overly romantic and overly simplistic, representing a new hybrid mix of the traditional Soto and Rinzai schools and Western psychoanalysis. Western Zen is thus thoroughly removed from the traditional life of the Japanese temple, where not only meditation, but also every manner of ritual practice would have been integral to the religion.

More recently, Tibetan Buddhism (also called Vajrayana) has gained prominence in the West. This is no doubt the result of the incredible personal charisma of the Dalai Lama. Many of the people responsible for the rising popularity of Tibetan Buddhism are themselves refugee Tibetan monks, but the forms of Buddhism they have shared with Westerners sometimes bear little resemblance to Vajrayana practices in Tibet. There

is, for instance, often a conscious downplaying of the complex ritual practices of Tibetan Buddhism, and a subsequent emphasis on the more "spiritual" dimensions of the religion. Certainly, it can be said that the
interest in and popularization of Zen and Tibetan Buddhism in America
and Europe is in part a response to frustrations about "organized" religion
in these contexts. There are, however, no easy explanations for the attraction of Buddhism in the West. The growth of these forms of Buddhism in the West, for instance, also must be seen in the larger context of
globalization.

On one level, the sort of hybridization that we see in Western versions
of Zen or Tibetan Buddhism is inevitable, but it is also important to see
this as part of the long history of Buddhism in the world. As much as
some Buddhists and scholars may want to preserve "original" Buddhism,
this is ultimately not only unrealistic, but also misguided. The Buddha
himself recognized that different contexts required different versions of
his teachings. Some people, he recognized, would be able to comprehend
the more technical and philosophical aspects of the *dharma*; for others,
however, a more basic mode of teaching was necessary. The Buddha thus
tailored his message to each particular audience. Buddhism has thus always been a fluid, changing religious tradition, and it continues to dy-
namically change in its many modern contexts. This is in no small degree
Buddhism's enduring appeal.

1. The head of the *Bodhisattva Maitreya*, Gandhara, Pakistan, 1st–2nd century
C.E. *Source*: Borromeo / Art Resource, New York.

2. The dream of Maya, from the balustrade of the *stupa* of Barhut, Madhya
Pradesh, India, 1st century B.C.E. Government Museum and National Art Gallery,
Madura, Tamil Nadu, India. *Source*: Borromeo / Art Resource, New York.

3. The Buddha preaching his first sermon at Sarnath, displaying the *dharmacakra mudra* (teaching gesture), 5th century C.E. Sarnath Museum, Uttar Pradesh, India. *Source*: Borromeo / Art Resource, New York.

4. The Mahabodhi temple, marking the sight of the Buddha's enlightenment at Bodhgaya, first constructed in the 6th century, with major renovations in the 19th century. Bodh Gaya, Bihar, India. *Source*: Borromeo / Art Resource, New York.

5. Mara attacking the Buddha after his enlightenment, 2nd–3rd century C.E. Gandhara, Pakistan. Museum fuer Indische Kunst, Staatliche Museenzu Berlin, Berlin, Germany. *Source*: Bildarchiv Preussischer Kulturbesitz / Art Resource, New York.

6. Limestone panel depicting the footprint of the Buddha (*buddhapada*), from the Great Stupa at Amaravati, 1st century B.C.E. British Museum, London, United Kingdom. Photo © British Library / HIP / Art Resource, New York.

7. Panel depicting the Buddha's passage out of this world, or *mahaparinirvana*. Gandhara, Pakistan, 2nd–3rd century C.E. British Museum, London, United Kingdom. *Source*: Erich Lessing / Art Resource, New York.

8. The Great Stupa at Sanchi, 1st century B.C.E. Madhya Pradesh, India. *Source*: Scala / Art Resource, New York.

9. *Siddhartha* emaciated after engaging in severe asceticism prior to his enlightenment, Gandhara, Pakistan, 2nd–3rd century C.E. Lahore Museum, Lahore, Pakistan. *Source*: Scala / Art Resource, New York.

10. Buddhist cave monastery at Ajanta, 1st century C.E. Maharashtra, India. *Source*: Scala / Art Resource, New York.

# BIOGRAPHICAL SKETCHES

## Ananda

The first cousin of the Buddha—said to have been born on the same day—and one of his most famous disciples. Ananda is said to have entered the *sangha* the year after the Buddha attained enlightenment. Initially, the Buddha did not have the same personal attendants at all times, but eventually declared that he was getting old and wanted a monk as his permanent companion, one who would respect his wishes in every way. Ananda was chosen because of his intense loyalty, and he accompanied the Buddha on most of his wanderings for over twenty-five years. Ananda is the Buddha's interlocutor in many canonical dialogues. He is also the key figure in an important episode recorded in the *Mahaparinibbana Sutta*, the Pali text in the *Digha Nikaya*, which records the Buddha's final days and his death. Upon learning of the Buddha's imminent death, Ananda is beside himself with grief, and worries that he will make no further progress on the Path without the Buddha as his teacher. The Buddha tells him that he should not grieve, that he should not be attached to the Buddha's person. Rather, the Buddha tells him that he has left his disciples the teachings, the *dharma*, which is all that they need to attain enlightenment.

In the list of disciples given in the *Anguttara Nikaya*, Ananda is mentioned five times, more than any other disciple, and is celebrated for his keen memory—which, according to the tradition, allows him to remember all of the Buddha's teachings—and his exemplary ethical conduct and service to others.

Ananda also played a key role in allowing women to become nuns (*bhikkhuni*). When Pajapati Gotami petitioned the Buddha to allow women to enter the *sangha*, the Buddha refused. When Ananda found them dejected at the Buddha's refusal, he went to the Buddha and asked him to grant the women's request. The Buddha refused, but Ananda did not give up. He asked three times, and each time the Buddha refused. Finally, he asked if women were even capable of making progress on the Path, and the Buddha said they were, and eventually changed his mind and allowed women to enter the *sangha*.

According to various sources, at the first Buddhist council, held shortly after the Buddha's death, Ananda had not yet attained enlightenment, and was thus initially excluded from the council. Ananda, however, applied himself with great vigor, and meditated until, much to the astonishment of the other monks, he attained enlightenment just prior to their meeting. At the first council, which was formed in order to record the Buddha's teachings, Ananda played a key role, chosen to recite large portions of the actual sermons, the *Dhamma Pitaka* portion of the Pali Canon, that the Buddha had delivered during his life. Ananda began each recitation with the phrase "Thus have I heard," to indicate that he was merely repeating the Buddha's teachings, exactly as he had heard them.

## Asanga

The founder of an important school of Mahayana Buddhism, the Yogacara, in the fourth century C.E. Asanga was born a Hindu, a member of a brahmin family in the North. He converted to Buddhism and became a monk of the Sarvastivada school. According to various legendary accounts, he soon left his monastery and began an intense meditational regime, focusing on Maitreya, hoping to gain a vision of the bodhisattva in order to receive direct teachings from him. He eventually gave up in frustration, though. As he was going down from the mountaintop, he realized that he had given up too easily, and returned. He repeated this same scenario several times until, eventually, having perfected both wisdom and compassion, he received a vision of the bodhisattva who taught him the Mahayana.

Historically, Asanga, along with his brother Vasubandhu, stands as one of the most important figures in Mahayana Buddhism, credited with rejuvenating Mahayana philosophy. He is said to have founded several monasteries and to have taken on dozens of pupils. Asanga is credited with writing a number of important commentaries on the *Perfection of*

*Wisdom* literature, and also with writing the *Yogacarabhumi-shastra*, the *Mahayana-samgraha*, and the *Abhidharma-samucaya*.

Asanga responded to what was seen as the tendency toward nihilism in Nagarjuna's Madhyamaka thought, with its intense emphasis on logic and absolute emptiness, and developed what would eventually be called the Yogacara school, which is also sometimes known as the "conscious-only" (Cittamatra) school. While the Madhyamaka philosophers insisted that no ultimately real thing could exist, Asanga asserted that only the mind is ultimately existent. Asanga and his followers defined three modes by which we perceive our world. First, through attached and erroneous discrimination, wherein things are incorrectly apprehended based on preconceptions; second, through the correct understanding of dependently originated nature of things; and third, by apprehending things as they truly are, independent of any other thing. This led to the important philosophical principle—influential in the development of Tibetan Buddhism and also Zen—of "mind-only," a theory according to which all existence is in fact nothing but an emanation of the human mind, of consciousness. Essentially, this means that human experience is nothing but false discriminations or imaginations.

## Ashoka

An Indian emperor of the Mauryan dynasty (third century B.C.E.), one of the greatest rulers of ancient India, he brought nearly all of India, together with Baluchistan and Afghanistan, under one sway for the first time in history. He converted to Buddhism, adopted the name Ashoka, and set out to transform his kingdom into one governed by *dharma*, by kindness, compassion, tolerance, and nonviolence.

Knowledge of Ashoka's rule comes from a large corpus of mythohistorical sources, as well as from the many pillars that he placed throughout his kingdom. These pillars were inscribed with ethical exhortations, known generally as "Ashoka's edicts," which reflect a Buddhist-informed policy of nonviolence, compassion, and tolerance. Ashoka had also built numerous Buddhist monasteries, shelters for Buddhist pilgrims, hospitals, and roads, and had also erected thousands of *stupas* throughout the Indian subcontinent.

Ashoka was instrumental in the spread of Buddhism. Not only did he establish monasteries and build *stupas* in India, but he also sent out

Buddhist missionaries throughout Asia, and as far away as Greece. His son, Mahinda, was sent to Sri Lanka and he established Buddhism there. Ashoka is also credited with calling the third Buddhist council, at his capital Pataliputra (modern Patna), during which the Pali Canon was formalized.

Perhaps the most enduring legacy of Ashoka's rule is the degree to which he still stands as the model Buddhist ruler. In Southeast Asia, in particular, Buddhist kings modeled themselves on Ashoka as the ultimate Dharmaraja, the righteous Buddhist king. Ashoka established the proper Buddhist king as one who gained his legitimacy from his support and adherence to Buddhism, and he laid out the close, symbiotic relationship between the king and the *sangha*: the king provided material goods, monasteries, and protection to the *sangha*; the *sangha*, in turn, provided the teachings and moral authority to the king. This close relationship between the ruler and Buddhism is still very much at play in many Southeast Asian countries, in which the king is considered not only a secular, but also a religious, leader.

## Buddhaghosa

One of the most prolific commentators on the Pali Canon. His works fill some thirty volumes, but little is actually known of his life and activities. According to the *Mahavamsa,* the mytho-historic chronicle of Sri Lanka, Buddhaghosa was born into a brahmin family near Bodhgaya, in northeast India, sometime around 400 C.E. He converted to Buddhism early in his life, and joined the *sangha*. As a monk, he gained considerable fame for his scholarly achievements. At the suggestion of one of his teachers, he traveled to Sri Lanka to study the Sinhalese commentaries on the Buddha's teachings. He took up residence at the Mahavihara monastery in Sri Lanka, and devoted his life to explicating the Pali Canon. He wrote on the *Vinaya* (monastic discipline), on the *Sutra* literature (the sayings of the Buddha), and also on the *Abhidharma* (higher philosophy). His commentaries became the standard for later Buddhists, and essentially defined the ways in which both monks and scholars have understood the texts of the Theravada school of Buddhism. Virtually all subsequent commentators on the Pali Canon were influenced by Buddhaghosa's interpretations.

The *Visuddhimagga* (The Path of Purity) is Buddhaghosa's most famous work, a book that remains the most influential of all Buddhist works. The *Visuddhimagga* is divided into three sections, roughly equivalent to the three divisions of the Path. It begins with a description and explication of *sila*, ethics or morality, then moves to a detailed discussion of *samadhi*, concentration or meditation, and then to an intricate analysis of *panna*, wisdom.

## Faxian

A Chinese monk of the Eastern Tsin dynasty, Faxian is said to have been born in 337 C.E. He was one of the first Chinese monks to travel to India as a pilgrim, travels that he recorded in great detail. He joined the *sangha* at the age of twenty, and became particularly focused on the *Vinaya* (the canon of monastic rules). He realized, however, that the texts available to him in China were incomplete, and set out to India in search of the full, authentic version of the *Vinaya*. He left his home in 399. Travel in ancient India was extremely difficult and dangerous, and it took Faxian some six years to reach India. Along the way, he visited the famous Dunhuang cave temples and many other important monuments. Faxian stayed in Khotan for three months, where he was especially impressed with the number of monasteries and the commitment of its Buddhist monks and laypeople. He then traveled to Gandhara, and then into northern India, which was at that time under Gupta rule. He arrived in Pataliputra in 405 and commenced studying Pali and Sanskrit Buddhist texts. He then traveled to eastern India, and eventually to Sri Lanka, finally returning home in 413.

He then settled in Nanking to begin translating the texts he had gathered, working on them until his death, sometime around 420. These texts helped establish Buddhism in China, providing a link between the Buddha's life in India (his homeland) and China, and served as authoritative transmissions of Buddhist doctrine. Of equal importance is the precedent that Faxian set for pilgrimage to India and to the places associated with important events in the Buddha's life. Faxian meticulously recorded his journeys in his *Record of the Buddhist Kingdoms*, a text that became the inspiration for later generations of Chinese pilgrims to India, notably Xuanzang (in the seventh century) and Yijing (635–713). These later pilgrims continued to bring canonical texts, commentaries, and new philosophical works back to China from India.

Faxian's accounts of his travels also provide a detailed description of early Buddhist practice in India (although his narrative is often interwoven with myth and fantastical hyperbole), and scholars of Buddhism have often relied upon them to provide insight into this period of Buddhist history in India.

## Maha Kassapa

One of the Buddha's closest early disciples. After the disciples Sariputta and Maha Moggallana died—before the Buddha himself—Maha Kassapa was held in greatest respect and reverence in the *sangha*. Several factors contributed to his high status: he was praised by the Buddha as being equal to him in significant respects; he bore seven of the thirty-two physical marks of the Great Being that the Buddha bore, and he had exchanged robes with the Buddha, a gesture of high respect. Maha Kassapa stands as the model ascetic, having lived a particularly disciplined and austere life. He was elected by the other monks to preside over the first Buddhist council. In China and Japan, Maha Kassapa became regarded as the first patriarch of Ch'an (Zen) Buddhism.

Like the Buddha's two chief disciples, Sariputta and Maha Moggallana, Maha Kassapa was born a brahmin, the son of a landowner in Magadha. He was called Pipphali, and grew up, like the Buddha, amid wealth and luxury. Even as a child, he showed signs of the ascetic life that he would later come to embody; he expressed his desire not to marry, and told his parents that he would take care of them as long as they lived, but after they died he would become an ascetic. His parents, however, repeatedly urged him to take a wife, and to comfort his mother, he agreed to marry. He told his parents, however, that he would only marry a perfect woman, and made a golden statue of a beautiful woman, clothed it in fine garments, and covered it in ornaments. "If you find me a woman like this," he told them, "I will remain a householder." His parents found such a woman, named Bhadda Kapilani, but it turned out that she, too, wished to renounce the world. The two were married, however, and lived several years together until, one day, Maha Kassapa came across a recently plowed field—a vision that parallels the Buddha's own—with worms being plucked up and eaten by birds. It occurred to him at this moment that his wealth was dependent on the suffering of other living beings, and he asked one of his laborers who would bear the karmic burden of this suffering, to which the man replied, "You yourself." At the same time, his wife had a nearly identical experience, and both decided to renounce their home life and become ascetics.

Maha Kassapa first met the Buddha after he and Bhadda Kapilani went there separate ways in search of enlightenment. On the road between Rajagriha and Nalanda, the Buddha sat down under a tree; when Kassapa arrived and saw the Buddha's radiance, he immediately recognized his enlightened status, and declared himself the Buddha's disciple. The two then set off to Rajagriha together, and along the way they stopped, and Maha Kassapa folded his robe fourfold for the Buddha to sit on. The Buddha remarked on how soft the robe was, and Maha Kassapa immediately offered it to him, taking his teacher's torn and ragged robe for his own, which became a mark of his dedication and ascetic rigor.

At the first council, Ananda mentioned that shortly before his death, the Buddha had said that it would be permitted to abolish some of the minor rules of discipline, but which rules, Ananda said he had not asked. Discussion followed, but the monks could not agree, at which point Maha Kassapa asked the assembly to consider that if they were to abolish rules arbitrarily, the lay followers would reproach them for being in a hurry to relax discipline so soon after the Buddha's death. Maha Kassapa thus suggested that the rules should be preserved intact without exception. He was thus held in great esteem by the other monks, and became the de facto head of the *sangha*. At the time of his death, he passed the Buddha's alms bowl—a powerful symbol of the continuity of the Buddha's teachings—to Ananda, who succeeded him as the most respected monk in the *sangha*.

## Maha Moggallana

One of the Buddha's chief disciples, along with Sariputta, with whom he is closely associated. He was born on the same day as Sariputta, near Rajagriha, in a prominent brahmin family. He was converted by Sariputta who, having heard a stanza from Assaji, shared it with his friend Moggallana, who became a Stream Winner. The two then went to visit the Buddha at Veluvana, where the Buddha preached to them, and they were ordained as monks. On the seventh day after his ordination, Maha Moggallana sat in meditation and was overcome by sleepiness; the Buddha, however, exhorted him to persevere, and he attained arahantship the following day. The Buddha announced to the *sangha* that he had chosen Moggallana and Sariputta as his chief disciples, much to the consternation of the other monks, who felt it unfair that two newcomers would be elevated to such lofty status. The Buddha told the assembled monks, however, that Maha Moggallana had worked diligently in his prior lives; he had previously been a householder named Sarada who gave away his wealth and became an ascetic. The Buddha had visited him in his hermitage, where Sarada and his seventy-four thousand pupils showed him great honor, and Sarada had made a vow that he would become the chief disciple of some future Buddha.

Maha Moggallana is declared to be the ideal disciple by the Buddha, whose example others should follow. In the "Saccavibhanga Sutta," for instance, the Buddha says that Moggallana and Sariputta are "twin brethren": "Sariputta is as she who brings forth and Moggallana is as the nurse of what is brought forth; Sariputta trains in the fruits of conversion, Moggallana trains in the highest good. Sariputta is able to teach and make plain the four Noble Truths; Moggallana, on the other hand, teaches by his special powers (*iddhi*)." With these powers, he could transform himself into any shape. When the Buddha and the other monks failed to receive alms in Veranja, Maha Moggallana offered to turn the world upside down so that the essence of the earth would come to the surface and serve as food. In another instance, the Buddha asked him to use his big toe to create an earthquake in order to frighten some monks who were talking idly in one of the monasteries. He also used his *iddhi* to subdue the evil naga Nandopananda.

Like Sariputta, Moggallana is celebrated in the Pali texts for his great wisdom. In one such instance, the Buddha preached to the Sakyans at Kapilavatthu, but wearied, asked Moggallana to instruct the monks on the finer points of the sermon. When the Buddha went to preach the *Abhidharma* in Tavatimsa, he asked Moggallana to preach to the people until his return.

Like Sariputta, Maha Moggallana died before the Buddha. According to the commentaries, his death was the result of a plot by the Niganthas. Moggallana had, during his life, used his powers to visit various worlds and returned to report that those who had followed the Buddha's teachings reached happy worlds, while the followers of heretics were reborn in hells. The heretics, seeing their numbers decreasing, bribed bandits to kill Moggallana. They caught and beat him, but he was able to drag himself to the Buddha to say goodbye before dying. Before passing into *nirvana*, however, he preached to the Buddha, and performed many miracles at his request.

## Maha Pajapati Gotami

According to the Pali tradition, Maha Pajapati Gotami (Maha Prajap-ati Gautami in Sanskrit) was Siddhartha's maternal aunt and foster mother. She is generally regarded as the first female monk, or *bhikkhuni*, and the founder of the first order of Buddhist nuns. According to this tra-dition, she began to practice the *dharma* that the Buddha taught, and at-tained the state of Stream Winner. The Buddha was visiting the town of Kapilavatthu in order to settle a dispute between the Sakiyans and the Koliyans, and there preached a sermon, the *Kalahavivada Sutta*. Upon hearing this sermon, five hundred young Sakiyan men joined the *sangha*, and their wives, led by Maha Pajapati, went to the Buddha and asked permission to be ordained as nuns. This Buddha refused, and went on to the town of Vesali. Pajapati and her companions, undaunted, had barbers shave their heads and put on monks' robes, and followed the Buddha on foot. They arrived bruised and cut and repeated their request. The Bud-dha again refused. This time, however, Maha Pajapati enlisted the help of the Buddha's chief disciple, Ananda, who petitioned the Buddha on her behalf. The Buddha finally agreed to allow the women to join the *sangha*, but specified that they would be required to adhere to eight additional rules, which stipulated that the nuns would be subordinate to the monks in matters of ordination and discipline.

According to the Pali tradition, after her ordination, Maha Pajapati went to the Buddha, who preached to her and gave her a special subject for meditation. She soon developed considerable insight into the *dharma*, and, along with five hundred companions, attained arahantship.

## Mahinda

The son of the great Indian king Ashoka, Mahinda was, according to the Theravada chronicles, twenty when he was ordained as a monk. He became an arahant the day he was ordained. When the third Buddhist council was held, Mahinda was chosen to lead a mission to Sri Lanka to convert the inhabitants of the island. He went along with six other monks, and there performed a variety of miracles and preached the *dharma*. As such, he is particularly important to the Theravada tradition in Sri Lanka. He is said to have met the king, Devanampiyatissa, and converted him to Buddhism by preaching the *Culahatthipadopama Sutta*.

Mahinda then showed the king various places that would become important to the growth of Buddhism in Sri Lanka. He described the different visits the Buddha had made to the island, and then helped Devanampiyatissa lay out the boundaries for the Mahavihara, the first and the largest monastery in Sri Lanka. In addition to the monks and various texts, Mahinda had brought relics of the Buddha to be kept on the island. Among these was the Buddha's collarbone, which was placed in the Thuparama—a huge *stupa* built just for the purpose. Mahinda also urged the king to send a party back to India to Ashoka to ask for a cutting of the Bodhi tree, which eventually was planted at Anuradhapura, and which, according to Sri Lankan tradition, still thrives. According to the chronicles, Mahinda is also said to have translated the commentaries on the Pali Canon into Sinhalese, and then taught them to the converted Sri Lankan monks.

## Nagarjuna

Often referred to as "the second Buddha" by Tibetan and East Asian Mahayana traditions of Buddhism, Nagarjuna proffered trenchant criticisms of Brahmanical and Buddhist substantialist philosophy, theory of knowledge, and approaches to practice. Nagarjuna's central concept of the "emptiness (*shunyata*) of all things (*dharmas*)," which pointed to the incessantly changing, and so never fixed, nature of all phenomena, served as much the terminological prop of subsequent Buddhist philosophical thinking as the vexation of opposed Vedic systems. The concept had fundamental implications for Indian philosophical models of causation, substance ontology, epistemology, conceptualizations of language, ethics and theories of world-liberating salvation, and proved seminal even for Buddhist philosophies in India, Tibet, China, and Japan, very different from Nagarjuna's own. Indeed, it would not be an overstatement to say that Nagarjuna's innovative concept of emptiness, though it was hermeneutically appropriated in many different ways by subsequent philosophers in both South and East Asia, was to profoundly influence the character of Buddhist thought.

Few details about Nagarjuna's life are known, although there are many legends about him. He may have been born in the second century C.E., in South India, near the town of Nagarjunakonda in modern Andhra Pradesh. According to traditional biographers, he was born into a brahmin family and later converted to Buddhism.

Nagarjuna knew the Pali Canon, and seems to have considered himself an adherent to the Theravada *Nikayas*, although he is often regarded as a Mahayana Buddhist. The most influential of his many texts is the *Mulamadhyamakakarika* (Fundamental Verses on the Middle Way), which contains the essence of his complex thought in twenty-seven chapters.

Although he is traditionally celebrated in the Mahayana as the founder of that school of Buddhism, it is doubtful that Nagarjuna saw himself as radically breaking with tradition. Rather, he was responding to and extending a number of debates within the *Abhidharma* philosophical context. Nagarjuna pushed the basic teachings of dependent origination (*pratityasamutpada*, in Sanskrit), and argued that since all things are ultimately empty of what he termed *svabhava*, or "own nature"—in line with the fundamental truth of "no self " taught by the Buddha—then all things must, logically, be empty of being. He also propounded that the Buddha employed the "two-truth" doctrine; there is an absolute truth, and a conventional truth that is employed to make known the absolute truth. Thus, people conventionally talk about a person, with a personality, when in fact no such person can absolutely exist, since he or she has no permanent self. Nagarjuna put forth the concept of *shunyata*, and pushed it to its logical extreme, essentially propounding a profoundly deconstructive philosophy, which broke down all attempts to understand the world in terms of fixed substances and essences.

Just as it is uncertain when and where he was born, it is unknown when exactly Nagarjuna died. Tibetan biographies say that when Nagarjuna's patron died, the new king, a brahmin, wanted a spiritual advisor more in keeping with his own religious tenets. He asked Nagarjuna to commit suicide out of compassion. Nagarjuna agreed, decapitating himself with a blade of holy grass.

## Padmasambhava (Guru Rinpoche)

Regarded by many Tibetans as the second Buddha, and considered to be an incarnation of the *dhyana* Buddha Amitabha, Padmasambhava is

credited with bringing Buddhism to Tibet in the ninth century C.E. Tibetan mytho-history holds that King Trisong Detsen invited Padmasambhava, then a monk in India, to Tibet in order to battle the demons who
had overrun the country.

As is the case with the Buddha, Padmasambhava's life story is punctu-
ated with myths and miracles. Traditional accounts of his life hold that
he was discovered by the ruler of a kingdom in northern India, who came
upon a large closed lotus—a prominent symbol for absolute purity and
enlightenment in Buddhism—in a lake. The lotus was marked with the
symbols of Amitabha, and blossomed to reveal an eight-year-old boy,
Padmasambhava (literally, "lotus born"). The king, Indrabhuti, adopted
him and raised him to become his successor, just as the historical Buddha
was raised. Like the Buddha, Padmasambhava too pursued a spiritual,
rather than political, path, despite his adopted father's wishes. He left the
palace and went off in search of enlightenment; in the course of his meditations, he developed great powers, such as the ability to instantly memorize any text, immortality, and invincibility.

According to the Tibetan tradition, Padmasambhava used his special
powers to subdue and convert the evil demons, redirecting their negative
energies to service in the *dharma*, a fundamental tenet of Tantra, or Vajrayana Buddhism. His journey through the Tibetan landscape, during
which he subdued and bound specific demons at specific places, has profound consequences for virtually all subsequent Tibetan Buddhists, deter-
mining the manner in which such demons—embodiments of negative
human emotions and energy—are perceived and treated in visualizations
and other ritual practices.

The Nyingma school of Tibetan Buddhism traces its origin to Padmasambhava. According to this tradition, Padmasambhava, upon seeing
that his followers were not yet ready to receive all of the many teachings
he had to reveal, hid hundreds of treasures—scriptures, images, and ritual
implements—throughout Tibet, including instructions for their revela-
tion for the benefit of future generations. The Nyingma school holds that
hundreds of masters have revealed the treasures over the centuries to
their disciples, thereby maintaining a direct link to Padmasambhava himself. In some monasteries, his life story is retold throughout the year, with
a particular incident recounted once in a month. In contemporary Tibet,
the story of Padmasambhava's life is known by virtually all Buddhists, and
painted and sculpted images of him are ubiquitous.

## Sariputta

Along with Maha Moggallana, Sariputta is generally regarded in the Pali sources as being one of the Buddha's chief disciples. He is celebrated not only for his wisdom, but also for his great compassion, particularly his willingness to administer to the ill. In the early *sangha*, Sariputta was declared by the Buddha to be the foremost possessor of wisdom, inferior only to himself. The Buddha would frequently merely suggest a topic, and Sariputta would preach a sermon on it in detail. The "Anupada Sutta" is, essentially, a long eulogy of Sariputta by the Buddha, who praises Sariputta as the supreme example of the perfect disciple, risen to mastery and perfection in noble virtue, noble concentration, noble perception, and noble deliverance.

As with many of the Buddha's early disciples, Sariputta was born a brahmin. The Pali tradition holds that he became a Stream Winner after hearing the first two lines of a sermon spoken by Assaji. He is said to have attained arahantship after hearing the Buddha preach the "Vedangaparig-gaha Sutta" in Rajagriha. Because he was held in such high regard by the Buddha, the purity and integrity of the *sangha* became Sariputta's special concern. Indeed, Sariputta was particularly meticulous concerning issues of *Vinaya*; a rule had been established, for instance, that a monk could only ordain one novice, and when a boy was sent to him for ordination from a particularly pious family, he refused to ordain the boy until the Buddha himself changed the rule.

In the Pali literature, Sariputta is described as being especially attached to Rahula, the Buddha's son. It is Sariputta who gives Rahula higher ordination, and trains him in meditation. Another story tells that when the Buddha's wife, Yasodhara, became ill, Rahula went to Sariputta who, because he was adept at caring for the ill, knew exactly what medicine to give her. There are several other instances in which Sariputta administers to the ill: for instance, when the layman Anathapindika became sick, Sariputta, along with Ananda, visited him and delivered the "Anathapindikovada Sutta." When Anathapindika died, he was reborn in the Tushita heaven as a result of the wisdom he had received.

Sariputta died some months before the Buddha. One story relates that when he realized his death was imminent, he took leave of the Buddha and returned to the village where he was born. There he found his mother, who professed no faith in the Buddha's teachings. Sariputta, however, out of his compassion, taught her the *dharma* as he lay dying, and she became a Stream Winner. He then called all of the other monks together, and asked if there was anything he had done to offend them over the last forty years. They assured him that there was nothing to forgive, and he attained *nirvana*.

## Vasubandhu

Along with his brother, Asanga, Vasubandhu is credited with founding the Yogacara school of Mahayana Buddhism in the fifth century. Vasubandhu was born in Gandhara, in northwest India, into a brahmin family. As a student, he astounded his teachers with his insightful mind. He entered the *sangha* and devoted himself to mastering Buddhist scholastics, particularly the Vaibhashika (or Sarvastivadin) *Abhidharma* literature. However, he began to see serious flaws in the logic of this *Abhidharma* corpus. Vasubandhu is said to have materially supported himself by lecturing on Buddhism; during the day he would lecture on Vaibhashika doctrine and in the evening condense the day's lectures into verses. These became the *Abhidharmakosha* (the Treasury of Abhidharma). When collected together, the six hundred plus verses gave a thorough summary of his entire philosophical system.

In the *Abhidharmakosha*, Vasubandhu analyzes seventy-five *dharmas*, the fundamental components of human experience. He divides them into various categories, offering detailed definitions of each one and examining their karmic interrelatedness as well as karmic qualities.

According to his biographers, Vasubandhu then spent several years traveling about South Asia, studying with various teachers. He apparently had little contact with his brother, Asanga, who had converted to the Mahayana school. According to the eighteenth-century Tibetan historian and biographer Bu-ston, Vasubandhu said as follows about his brother and his philosophical leanings: "Alas, Asanga, residing in the forest, has practised meditation for twelve years. Without having attained anything by this meditation, he has founded a system, so difficult and burdensome, that it can be carried only by an elephant." Asanga, however, expounded to his brother the superior teachings of the Mahayana, and Vasubandhu converted. He then began composing a series of commentaries on crucial Mahayana texts: on the *Akshayamatinirdesha* and *Dashabhumika Sutras*, on the *Avatamsaka Sutra*, the *Mahayanasamgraha*, the *Nirvana Sutra*, and the

*Vimalakirtinirdesha* and *Shrimaladevi Sutras*. He received patronage from two Gupta rulers in India, Skandagupta (455–467 C.E.) and Narasimhagupta (467–473 C.E.). He was celebrated as a great debater, in particular, to the point that the ruler Chandragupta II is said to have rewarded him with 300,000 gold coins for victory in a debate over the Samkhyas. According to his biographers, Vasubandhu used this money to build three monasteries, one for the Mahayanists, one for the Sarvastivadins, and one for nuns.

Vasubandhu has been one of the most influential of all Mahayana thinkers. After Nagarjuna's writings, Vasubandhu's extensive commentaries are among the most important Mahayana Buddhist texts, and continue to be essential in the training of monks, throughout the Buddhist world. In that text, Vasubandhu articulates an extremely important Yogacara point, that since without consciousness nothing can be apprehended, it is therefore consciousness that is the necessary condition for existence. Thus, from the Yogacara perspective, what we believe to be external objects are actually nothing more than mental projections, and so what we think, know, conceptualize, or experience, all really only occur to us in our consciousness, and nowhere else. Vasubandhu's philosophical writings became essential texts in the formation of not only Tibetan Buddhism, but also the Pure Land and Ch'an/Zen schools in China and Japan. Indeed, he came to be regarded as a bodhisattva in some traditions in India, China, and Tibet.

## Xuanzang

Perhaps best known for his seventeen-year pilgrimage to India, Xuanzang, along with the earlier pilgrim Faxian, was instrumental in transmitting Buddhism from India to China. Born in 602, he was the youngest of four children, the son of a conservative Confucianist. According to traditional biographies, as a child, Xuanzang possessed a keen intellect in and dedication to Confucian principles. After the death of his father in 611, Xuanzang lived for five years in the Jingtu monastery in Luoyang, where he studied the various schools of Buddhism and the *Abhidharma* philosophical systems. He asked to be admitted to the *sangha* at thirteen, and although the monastic rules prohibited his ordination because of his age, the abbot Zheng Shanguo made an exception in his case because of his remarkable intellect and diligence.

In 629, Xuanzang embarked on his pilgrimage to India, which he meticulously recorded in *Records of the Western Regions of the Great T'ang Dynasty*. He began his journey by crossing the Gobi desert, and then traveling southwest into central Asia. He visited dozens of monasteries, including all of the major sites associated with the life story of the Buddha. He studied the scriptures of the Theravada and Mahayana schools at these monasteries with some of the India's greatest intellects. In Taxila, a Mahayana kingdom in what is now modern Kashmir, he encountered 5,000 monks living in 100 monasteries. He stayed there for two years, from 631 to 633, studying various texts. While there, the fourth Buddhist council, called by King Kanishka of Kushana dynasty, took place, an event Xuanzang records in his writings.

He then traveled further in India, collecting texts and images to take back to China. In particular, he spent two years at the great Buddhist university Nalanda in northeastern India, where he studied Sanskrit, logic, grammar, and Brahmana philosophy, and particularly the teachings of the Yogacara school. According to some accounts of his life, the great Buddhist scholar Silabhadra (529–645) was then the abbot of Nalanda, and was contemplating suicide after years of debilitating illness. However, in a dream he received instructions to endure suffering and await the arrival of a Chinese monk in order to guarantee the preservation of the Mahayana tradition abroad. Indeed, Xuanzang became Silabhadra's disciple and in 636 was initiated into the Yogacara. When he finally returned to China, he brought with him over 650 Sanskrit texts, and, with the support of the emperor, set up a large translation center, drawing students and scholars from all over East Asia. He is credited with translating over 1,300 scriptures into Chinese. Most closely aligned with the Yogacara philosophical tradition, Xuanzang founded the Faxiang school of Buddhism, which, although short lived, was influential in the development of later Chinese schools of Buddhism. Xuanzang's journey, and the legends that grew up around it, inspired one of the great classics of Chinese literature, the Ming-period novel *Journey to the West*.

# PRIMARY DOCUMENTS

## DOCUMENT 1

*The following is taken from the Pali Canon, from the* Digha Nikaya *account of the Buddha's life in the palace. This passage is one of the best known in all of Buddhist literature—although there are many variations of the story, with slightly different details—and relates Siddhartha's encounter with "the four sights." In the passage, the prince convinces his chariot driver to take him outside of the walls of the palace—which represents a kind of fantasyland where there is nothing unpleasant—where he faces reality for the first time. The sights that he encounters are an old man, a sick person, a corpse, and a monk. Through these four encounters Siddhartha realizes that youth and health, and even life itself, are only temporary, and that in fact the world is characterized by impermanence, which engenders suffering. He also realizes that the only way out of this suffering is to find and follow a correct religious path—as represented by the monk he comes across.*

Now the young lord Gautama, when many days had passed by, bade his charioteer make ready the state carriages, saying: "Get ready the carriages, good charioteer, and let us go through the park to inspect the pleasaunce." "Yes, my lord," replied the charioteer, and harnessed the state carriages and sent word to Gautama: "The carriages are ready, my lord; do now what you deem fit." Then Gautama mounted a state carriage and drove out in state into the park.

Now the young lord saw, as he was driving to the park, an aged man as bent as a roof gable, decrepit, leaning on a staff, tottering as he walked, afflicted and long past his prime. And seeing him Gautama said: "That man, good charioteer, what has he done, that his hair is not like that of other men, nor his body?"

"He is what is called an aged man, my lord."

"But why is he called aged?"

"He is called aged, my lord, because he has not much longer to live."

"But then, good charioteer, am I too subject to old age, one who has not got past old age?"

"You, my lord, and we too, we all are of a kind to grow old; we have not got past old age."

"Why then, good charioteer, enough of the park for today. Drive me back hence to my rooms."

"Yea, my lord," answered the charioteer, and drove him back. And he, going to his rooms, sat brooding sorrowful and depressed, thinking, "Shame then verily be upon this thing called birth, since to one born old age shows itself like that!"

Thereupon the raja sent for the charioteer and asked him: "Well, good charioteer, did the boy take pleasure in the park? Was he pleased with it?"

"No, my lord, he was not."

"What then did he see on his drive?"

(And the charioteer told the raja all.)

Then the raja thought thus: We must not have Gautama declining to rule. We must not have him going forth from the house into the homeless state. We must not let what the brahman soothsayers spoke of come true.

So, that these things might not come to pass, he let the youth be still more surrounded by sensuous pleasures. And thus Gautama continued to live amidst the pleasures of sense.

Now after many days had passed by, the young lord again bade his charioteer make ready and drove forth as once before. . . .

And Gautama saw, as he was driving to the park, a sick man, suffering and very ill, fallen and weltering in his own water, by some being lifted up, by others being dressed. Seeing this, Gautama asked: "That man, good charioteer, what has he done that his eyes are not like others' eyes, nor his voice like the voice of other men?" "He is what is called ill, my lord."

"But what is meant by ill?"

"It means, my lord, that he will hardly recover from his illness."

"But I am too, then, good charioteer, subject to fall ill; have I not got out of reach of illness?"

"You, my lord, and we too, we are all subject to fall ill; we have not got beyond the reach of illness."

"Why then, good charioteer, enough of the park for today. Drive me back hence to my rooms." "Yea, my lord," answered the charioteer, and drove him back. And he, going to his rooms, sat brooding sorrowful and depressed, thinking: Shame then verily be upon this thing called birth, since to one born decay shows itself like that, disease shows itself like that. . . .

Now once again, after many days the young lord Gautama . . . drove forth.

And he saw, as he was driving to the park, a great concourse of people clad in garments of different colors constructing a funeral pyre. And seeing this he asked his charioteer: "Why now are all those people come together in garments of different colors, and making that pile?"

"It is because someone, my lord, has ended his days."

"Then drive the carriage close to him who has ended his days." "Yea, my lord," answered the charioteer, and did so. And Gautama saw the corpse of him who had ended his days and asked: "What, good charioteer, is ending one's days?"

"It means, my lord, that neither mother, nor father, nor other kinsfolk will now see him, nor will he see them."

"But am I too then subject to death, have I not got beyond reach of death? Will neither the raja, nor the ranee, nor any other of my kin see me more, or shall I again see them?"

"You, my lord, and we too, we are all subject to death; we have not passed beyond the reach of death. Neither the raja, nor the ranee, nor any other of your kin will see you any more, nor will you see them."

"Why then, good charioteer, enough of the park for today. Drive me back hence to my rooms."

"Yea, my lord," replied the charioteer, and drove him back.

And he, going to his rooms, sat brooding sorrowful and depressed, thinking: Shame verily be upon this thing called birth, since to one born the decay of life, since disease, since death shows itself like that. . . .

Thereupon the raja questioned the charioteer as before and as before let Gautama be still more surrounded by sensuous enjoyment. And thus he continued to live amidst the pleasures of sense.

Now once again, after many days . . . the lord Gautama . . . drove forth.

And he saw, as he was driving to the park, a shaven-headed man, a recluse, wearing the yellow robe. And seeing him he asked the charioteer, "That man, good charioteer, what has he done that his head is unlike other men's heads and his clothes too are unlike those of others?" "That is what they call a recluse, because, my lord, he is one who has gone forth."

"What is that, 'to have gone forth'?"

"To have gone forth, my lord, means being thorough in the religious life, thorough in the peaceful life, thorough in good action, thorough in meritorious conduct, thorough in harmlessness, thorough in kindness to all creatures."

"Excellent indeed, friend charioteer, is what they call a recluse, since so thorough in his conduct in all those respects, wherefore drive me up to that forthgone man."

"Yea, my lord," replied the charioteer and drove up to the recluse. Then Gautama addressed him, saying, "You master, what have you done that your head is not as other men's heads, nor your clothes as those of other men?"

"I, my lord, am one whose has gone forth."

"What, master, does that mean?"

"It means, my lord, being thorough in the religious life, thorough in the peaceful life, thorough in good actions, thorough in meritorious conduct, thorough in harmlessness, thorough in kindness to all creatures."

"Excellently indeed, master, are you said to have gone forth since so thorough is your conduct in all those respects." Then the lord Gautama bade his charioteer, saying: "Come then, good charioteer, do you take the carriage and drive it back hence to my rooms. But I will even here cut off my hair, and don the yellow robe, and go forth from the house into the homeless state."

"Yea, my lord," replied the charioteer, and drove back. But the prince Gautama, there and then cutting off his hair and donning the yellow robe, went forth from the house into the homeless state.

Now at Kapilavatthu, the raja's seat, a great number of persons, some eighty-four thousand souls, heard of what prince Gautama had done and thought: Surely this is no ordinary religious rule, this is no common going forth, in that prince Gautama himself has had his head shaved and has donned the yellow robe and has gone forth from the house into the homeless state. If prince Gautama has done this, why then should not we also? And they all had their heads shaved and donned the yellow robes, and in imitation of the Bodhisat they went forth from the house into the homeless state. So the Bodhisat went up on his rounds through the villages, towns and cities accompanied by that multitude.

Now there arose in the mind of Gautama the Bodhisat, when he was meditating in seclusion, this thought: That indeed is not suitable for me that I should live beset. 'Twere better were I to dwell alone, far from the crowd.

So after a time he dwelt alone, away from the crowd. Those eighty-four thousand recluses went one way, and the Bodhisat went another way.

Now there arose in the mind of Gautama the Bodhisat, when he had gone to his place and was meditating in seclusion, this thought: Verily, this world has fallen upon trouble—one is born, and grows old, and dies, and falls from one state, and springs up in another. And from the suffering, moreover, no one knows of any way of escape, even from decay and death. O, when shall a way of escape from this suffering be made known—from decay and from death?

*Source*: Translated by Earl H. Brewster, in *The Life of Gautama Buddha*. New York: Kegan Paul, Trench, Trübner, 1926.

# DOCUMENT 2

*The following is taken from the* Buddhacarita, *a first-century-C.E. biography of the Buddha written by the Indian Buddhist Ashvaghosha. This passage recounts the process of Prince Siddhartha's decision to abandon his life of privilege in his father's palace. Two things, in particular, motivate him to do so: first, his encounter with the suffering, or* dukkha, *that characterizes human existence; and, second, his encounter with the* shramana, *the wandering ascetic who is seeking an end to this suffering. In this version of the story, Siddhartha leaves the palace in the middle of the night, and sets out to seek enlightenment, not, the passage emphasizes, simply for himself, but for all beings.*

## Canto V

### Flight

1. Though the son of the Sakya king was thus tempted by priceless objects of sense, he felt no contentment, he obtained no relief, like a lion pierced deeply in the heart by a poisoned arrow.

2. Then longing for spiritual peace, he set forth outside with the king's permission in order to see the forest, and for companions he had a retinue of ministers' sons, chosen for their reliability and skill in converse.

3. He went out, mounted on the good horse Kanthaka, the bells of whose bit were of fresh gold and whose golden trappings were beautified with waving chowries, and so he resembled a *karnikara* emblem mounted on a flagpole.

4. Desire for the forest as well as the excellence of the land led him on to the more distant jungle-land, and he saw the soil being ploughed, with its surface broken with the tracks of the furrows like waves of water.

5. When he saw the ground in this state, with the young grass torn up and scattered by the ploughs and littered with dead worms, insects and other creatures, he mourned deeply as at the slaughter of his own kindred.

6. And as he observed the ploughmen with their bodies discoloured by wind, dust and the sun's rays, and the oxen in distress with the labour of drawing, the most noble one felt extreme compassion.

7. Then alighting from his horse, he walked slowly over the ground, overcome with grief. And as he considered the coming into being and the passing away of creation, he cried in his affliction, "How wretched this is."

8. And desiring to reach perfect clearness with his mind, he stopped his friends who were following him, and proceeded himself to a solitary spot at the root of a jambu-tree, whose beautiful leaves were waving in all directions.

9. And there he sat down on the clean ground, with grass bright like beryl; and reflecting on the origin and destruction of creation he took the path of mental stillness.

10. And his mind at once came to a stand and at the same time he was freed from mental troubles such as desire for the objects of sense etc. And he entered into the first trance of calmness which is accompanied by gross and subtle cogitation and which is supermundane in quality.

11. Then he obtained possession of concentration of mind, which springs from discernment and yields extreme ecstasy and bliss, and thereafter, rightly perceiving in his mind the course of the world, he meditated on this same matter.

12. "A wretched thing it is indeed that man, who is himself helpless and subject to the law of old age, disease and destruction, should in his ignorance and the blindness of his conceit, pay no heed to another who is the victim of old age, disease or death.

13. For if I, who am myself such, should pay no heed to another whose nature is equally such, it would not be right or fitting in me, who have knowledge of this, the ultimate law."

14. As he thus gained correct insight into the evils of disease, old age and death, the mental intoxication relating to the self, which arises from belief in one's strength, youth and life, left him in a moment.

15. He did not rejoice nor yet was he downcast; doubt came not over him, nor sloth, nor drowsiness. And he felt no longing for sensual pleasures, no hatred or contempt for others. . . .

43. As the day departed then, he mounted, blazing like the sun with his beauty, to his palace, even as the rising sun climbs Meru, in order to dispel the darkness with the splendour of his self.

44. Going up to a chamber which was filled with incense of the finest black aloe and, had lighted candelabra glittering with gold, he repaired to a splendid golden couch inlaid with streaks of diamond.

45. Then the noblest of women waited with musical instruments on him, the noblest of men, the peer of Indra, just as the troops of Apsarases wait on the son of the Lord of Wealth on the moon-white summit of Himavat.

46. But even those splendid instruments, like though they were to the music of the gods, failed to delight or thrill him; the one desire of the saintly prince was to leave his house in search of the bliss of the highest good, and therefore he did not rejoice.

47. Thereon the Akanistha deities, supreme in austerities, taking cognisance of his resolve, all at once brought sleep there over the women and distorted the gestures of their limbs.

48. So one, as she lay there, supported her cheek on an unsteady hand, and, as if angry, abandoned the flute in her lap, dear though it was to her, with its decoration of gold leaf. . . .

57. Others, though really large-eyed and fair-browed, showed no beauty with their eyes shut, like lotus-beds with their flowerbuds closed at the setting of the sun.

58. Another too had her hair loose and dishevelled, and with the ornaments and clothes fallen from her hips and her necklaces scattered she lay like an image of a woman broken by an elephant.

59. But others, helplessly lost to shame despite their natural decorum and endowment of excellent beauty, lay in immodest attitudes, snoring, and stretched their limbs, all distorted and tossing their arms about.

60. Others looked ugly, lying unconscious like corpses, with their ornaments and garlands cast aside, the fastening knots of their dresses undone, and eyes moveless with the whites showing.

61. Another lay as if sprawling in intoxication, with her mouth gaping wide, so that the saliva oozed forth, and with her limbs spread out so as to show what should have been hid. Her beauty was gone, her form distorted. . . .

63. When the king's son saw the young women lying in these different ways and looking so loathsome with their uncontrolled movements, though ordinarily their forms were beautiful, their speech agreeable, he was moved to disgust:—

64. "Such is the real nature of woman in the world of the living, impure and loathsome; yet man, deceived by dress and ornaments, succumbs to passion for women.

65. If man were to consider the natural form of woman and such a transformation produced in her by sleep, most certainly his heedlessness in respect of her would not increase; yet, overcome by his impressions of her excellence, he succumbs to passion."

66. Thus he recognized the difference and there arose in him a desire to escape that night. Then the gods, understanding his purpose, caused the doors of the palace to fly open. . . .

83. Then he went forth out of his father's city, in the firmness of his resolve quitting without concern his father, who was devoted to him, his young son, his affectionate people and his unequalled magnificence.

84. Thereon he, whose eyes were long like stainless lotuses born of the mud, looked back at the city and uttered a lion-roar: "I shall not be entering the city named after Kapila, till I have seen the further shore of life and death."

85. Hearing his words, the troops of the court of the Lord of Wealth rejoiced, and the hosts of gods with joyful minds foretold the fulfillment of his resolve.

86. Other heavenly beings of fiery forms recognized his purpose to be of the greatest difficulty and, like moon beams piercing a rift in a cloud, produced a bright light on his frosty path.

87. But that steed, like a steed of the Sun, speeding on as if spurred in mind, and the prince traveled very many leagues, before the stars in the sky grew discolored with the dawn.

Source: *Buddhacarita: The Great Departure*. Translated by Samuel Beal. Sacred Books of the East, vol. 19. Oxford: Oxford University Press, 1883.

# DOCUMENT 3

*During his quest for enlightenment, Shakyamuni experimented with various modes of extreme austerities, to the point that he had nearly starved to death. A young woman, Sujata, came upon him in this emaciated state, and offered him a portion of rice gruel. Having taken in this modest nourishment, Shakyamuni sat underneath the Bodhi tree in meditation, having vowed not to move until he attained enlightenment. Hearing this vow, the evil being Mara, the Buddhist manifestation of death and desire, felt threatened. The source of Mara's power over beings was rooted in their attachment to sensuous pleasures and their fear of death. If Siddhartha could attain freedom from these attachments, which would lead to enlightenment, then Mara would lose his control over him and other beings who would follow in the Buddha's path. Mara thus unleashed a series of illusionary temptations to try to distract Siddhartha. All through these tribulations, however, the Buddha-to-be sat calmly and Mara, defeated, withdrew.*

## Defeat of Mara

1. When the great sage, the scion of a line of royal seers, sat down there, after making his vow for liberation, the world rejoiced, but Mara, the enemy of the good Law, trembled.

2. Him whom in the world they call the God of Love, him of the bright weapon and also the flower-arrowed, that same one, as the monarch of the activities of the passions and as the enemy of liberation, they style Mara.

3. His three sons, Caprice, Gaiety and Wantonness, and his three daughters, Discontent, Delight and Thirst, asked him why he was depressed in mind, and he answered them thus:—

4. "The sage, wearing the armour of his vow and drawing the bow of resolution with the arrow of wisdom, sits yonder, desiring to conquer my realm; hence this despondency of my mind.

5. For if he succeeds in overcoming me and expounds to the world the path of final release, then is my realm to-day empty, like that of the Videha king, when he fell from good conduct.

6. While therefore he has not yet attained spiritual eyesight and is still within my sphere, I shall go to break his vow, like the swollen current of a river breaking an embankment."

7. Then, seizing his flower-made bow and his five world-deluding arrows, he, the causer of unrest to mortal minds, approached the *asvattha* tree accompanied by his children.

8. Next Mara placed his left hand on the tip of the bow and, fingering the arrow, thus addressed the sage, who was tranquilly seated in his desire to cross to the further shore of the ocean of existence:—

9. "Up, up, Sir Ksatriya, afraid of death. Follow your own *dharma*, give up the *dharma* of liberation. Subdue the world both with arrows and with sacrifices, and from the world obtain the world of Vasava.

10. For this is the path to issue forth by, the famous one travelled by kings of olden time. It is ignominious for one born in a renowned family of royal seers to practise this mendicancy.

11. Or if, O firm in purpose, you do not rise up to-day, be steadfast, do not give up your vow. For this arrow that I have ready is the very one I discharged at Surpaka, the fishes' foe.

12. And at the mere touch of it the son of Ida, though he was the grandson of the moon, fell into a frenzy, and Santanu lost his self-control. How much more then would anyone else do so, who is weak with the decadence of the present age?

13. So rise up quickly and recover your senses; for this ever-destructive arrow stands ready. I do not discharge it at those who are given to sensual pleasures and show compliance to their mistresses, any more than I would at sheldrakes."

14. Despite these words the sage of the Sakyas showed no concern and did not change his posture; so then Mara brought forward his sons and daughters and discharged the arrow at him.

15. But even when the arrow was shot at him, he paid no heed to it and did not falter in his firmness. . . .

18. Then as soon as Mara thought of his army in his desire to obstruct the tranquillity of the Sakya sage, his followers stood round him, in various forms and carrying lances, trees, javelins, clubs and swords in their hands;

19. Having the faces of boars, fishes, horses, asses and camels, or the countenances of tigers, bears, lions and elephants, one-eyed, many-mouthed, three-headed, with pendulous bellies and speckled bellies;

20. Without knees or thighs, or with knees vast as pots, or armed with

tusks or talons, or with skulls for faces, or with many bodies, or with half their faces broken off or with huge visages;

21. Ashy-grey in colour, tricked out with red spots, carrying ascetics' staves, with hair smoke-coloured like a monkey's, hung round with garlands, with pendent ears like elephants, clad in skins or entirely naked;

22. With half their countenances white or half their bodies green; some also copper-colored, smoke-colored, tawny or black; some too with arms having an overgarment of snakes, or with rows of jangling bells at their girdles;

23. Tall as toddy-palms and grasping stakes, or of the stature of children with projecting tusks, or with the faces of sheep and the eyes of birds, or with cat-faces and human bodies;

24. With disheveled hair, or with topknots and half-shaven polls, clothed in red and with disordered headdresses, with bristling faces and frowning visages, suckers of the vital essence and suckers of the mind.

25. Some, as they ran, leapt wildly about, some jumped on each other; while some gamboled in the sky, others sped along among the treetops.

26. One danced about, brandishing a trident; another snorted, as he trailed a club; one roared like a bull in his excitement, another blazed fire from every hair.

27. Such were the hordes of fiends who stood encompassing the root of the *bodhi* tree on all sides, anxious to seize and to kill, and awaiting the command of their master. . . .

33. But when the great seer beheld Mara's army standing as a menace to that method of *dharma*, like a lion seated amidst kine he did not quail nor was he at all perturbed.

34. Then Mara gave orders to his raging army of demons for terrifying the sage. Thereon that army of his resolved to break down his steadfastness with their various powers.

35. Some stood trying to frighten him, their many tongues hanging out flickering, their teeth sharp-pointed, their eyes like the sun's orb, their mouths gaping, their ears sticking up stiff as spikes.

36. As they stood there in such guise, horrible in appearance and manner, he was no more alarmed by them or shrank before them than before over-excited infants at play. . . .

56. Then a certain being of high station and invisible form, standing in the sky and seeing that Mara was menacing the seer and without cause of enmity was displaying wrath, addressed him with imperious voice.

57. "Mara, you should not toil to no purpose, give up your murderous intent and go in peace. For this sage can no more be shaken by you than Meru, greatest of mountains, by the wind.

58. Fire might lose its nature of being hot, water its liquidity, earth its solidity, but in view of the meritorious deeds accumulated by him through many ages he cannot abandon his resolution.

59. For such is his vow, his energy, his psychic power, his compassion for creation, that he will not rise up till he has attained the truth, just as the thousand-rayed sun does not rise without dispelling the darkness. . . ."

70. And when Mara heard that speech of his and observed the great sage's unshakenness, then, his efforts frustrated, he went away dejectedly with the arrows by which the world is smitten in the heart.

71. Then his host fled away in all directions, its elation gone, its toil rendered fruitless, its rocks, logs and trees scattered everywhere, like a hostile army whose chief has been slain by the foe.

72. As he of the flower-banner fled away defeated with his following, and the great seer, the passion-free conqueror of the darkness of ignorance, remained victorious, the heavens shone with the moon like a maiden with a smile, and there fell a rain of sweet-smelling flowers filled with water.

*Source: Buddhacarita: The Great Departure.* Translated by Samuel Beal. Sacred Books of the East, vol. 19. Oxford: Oxford University Press, 1883.

# DOCUMENT 4

*After the Buddha had attained enlightenment under the Bodhi tree at Bodhgaya, he was hesitant to share the wisdom that he had realized, fearful that it would confuse his disciples rather than enlighten them. He is convinced, though, by Brahma and the other Hindu gods to share the* dharma *so that they, the gods, as well as all humans, can also obtain release from* samsara. *His first sermon is called, in Pali, the* Dhammacakkapavattana Sutta, *literally, the "turning of the wheel of* dharma." *In this first sermon, the Buddha lays out the basic foundation of the Eightfold Path and the Four Noble Truths.*

Reverence to the Blessed One, the Holy One, the Fully-Enlightened One.

1. Thus have I heard. The Blessed One was once staying at Benares, at the hermitage called Migadaya. And there the Blessed One addressed the company of the five Bhikkhus, and said:

2. "There are two extremes, O Bhikkhus, which the man who has given up the world ought not to follow—the habitual practice, on the one hand of those things whose attraction depends upon the passions, and especially of sensuality—a low and pagan way (of seeking satisfaction) unworthy, unprofitable, and fit only for the worldly-minded—and the habitual practice, on the other hand, of asceticism (or self-mortification), which is painful, unworthy, and unprofitable.

3. "There is a middle path, O Bhikkhus, avoiding these two extremes, discovered by the Tathagata—a path which opens the eyes, and bestows understanding, which leads to peace of mind, to the higher wisdom, to full enlightenment, to Nirvana!

4. "What is that middle path, O Bhikkhus, avoiding these two extremes, discovered by the Tathagata—that path which opens the eyes, and bestows understanding, which leads to peace of mind, to the higher wisdom, to full enlightenment, to Nirvana? Verily! it is this noble eightfold path; that is to say:

Right views;
Right aspirations;
Right speech;
Right conduct;
Right livelihood;
Right effort;
Right mindfulness;
and Right contemplation.

"This, O Bhikkhus, is that middle path, avoiding these two extremes, discovered by the Tathagata—that path which opens the eyes, and bestows understanding which leads to peace of mind, to the higher wisdom, to full enlightenment, to Nirvana!

5. "Now this, O Bhikkhus, is the noble truth concerning suffering.

"Birth is attended with pain, decay is painful, disease is painful, death is painful. Union with the unpleasant is painful, painful is separation from the pleasant; and any craving that is unsatisfied, that too is painful. In brief, the five aggregates which spring from attachment (the conditions of individuality and their cause) are painful.

"This then, O Bhikkhus, is the noble truth concerning suffering.

6. "Now this, O Bhikkhus, is the noble truth concerning the origin of suffering.

"Verily, it is that thirst (or craving), causing the renewal of existence, accompanied by sensual delight, seeking satisfaction now here, now there—that is to say, the craving for the gratification of the passions, or the craving for (a future) life, or the craving for success (in this present life).

"This then, O Bhikkhus, is the noble truth concerning the origin of suffering.

7. "Now this, O Bhikkhus, is the noble truth concerning the destruction of suffering.

"Verily, it is the destruction, in which no passion remains, of this very thirst; the laying aside of, the getting rid of, the being free from, the harboring no longer of this thirst.

"This then, O Bhikkhus, is the noble truth concerning the destruction of suffering.

8. "Now this, O Bhikkhus, is the noble truth concerning the way which leads to the destruction of sorrow. Verily! it is this noble eightfold path; that is to say:

Right views;
Right aspirations;
Right speech;
Right conduct;
Right livelihood;
Right effort;
Right mindfulness;
and Right contemplation.

"This then, O Bhikkhus, is the noble truth concerning the destruction of sorrow.

9. "That this was the noble truth concerning sorrow, was not, O Bhikkhus, among the doctrines handed down, but there arose within me the eye (to perceive it), there arose the knowledge (of its nature), there arose the understanding (of its cause), there arose the wisdom (to guide in the path of tranquillity), there arose the light (to dispel darkness from it).

10. "And again, O Bhikkhus, that I should comprehend that this was the noble truth concerning sorrow, though it was not among the doc-

trines handed down, there arose within me the eye, there arose the knowledge, there arose the understanding, there arose the wisdom, there arose the light.

11. "And again, O Bhikkhus, that I had comprehended that this was the noble truth concerning sorrow, though it was not among the doctrines handed down, there arose within me the eye, there arose the knowledge, there arose the understanding, there arose the wisdom, there arose the light.

12. "That this was the noble truth concerning the origin of sorrow, though it was not among the doctrines handed down, there arose within me the eye; but there arose within me the knowledge, there arose the understanding, there arose the wisdom, there arose the light.

13. "And again, O Bhikkhus, that I should put away the origin of sorrow, though the noble truth concerning it was not among the doctrines handed down, there arose within me the eye, there arose the knowledge, there arose the understanding, there arose the wisdom, there arose the light.

14. "And again, O Bhikkhus, that I had fully put away the origin of sorrow, though the noble truth concerning it was not among the doctrines handed down, there arose within me the eye, there arose the knowledge, there arose the understanding, there arose the wisdom, there arose the light.

15. "That this, O Bhikkhus, was the noble truth concerning the destruction of sorrow, though it was not among the doctrines handed down; but there arose within me the eye, there arose the knowledge, there arose the understanding, there arose the wisdom, there arose the light.

16. "And again, O Bhikkhus, that I should fully realize the destruction of sorrow, though the noble truth concerning it was not among the doctrines handed down, there arose within me the eye, there arose the knowledge, there arose the understanding, there arose the wisdom, there arose the light.

17. "And again, O Bhikkhus, that I had fully realized the destruction of sorrow, though the noble truth concerning it was not among the doctrines handed down, there arose within me the eye, there arose the knowledge, there arose the understanding, there arose the wisdom, there arose the light.

18. "That this was the noble truth concerning the way which leads

to the destruction of sorrow, was not, O Bhikkhus, among the doctrines handed down; but there arose within me the eye, there arose the knowledge, there arose the understanding, there arose the wisdom, there arose the light.

19. "And again, O Bhikkhus, that I should become versed in the way which leads to the destruction of sorrow, though the noble truth concerning it was not among the doctrines handed down, there arose within me the eye, there arose the knowledge, there arose the understanding, there arose the wisdom, there arose the light.

20. "And again, O Bhikkhus, that I had become versed in the way which leads to the destruction of sorrow, though the noble truth concerning it was not among the doctrines handed down, there arose within me the eye, there arose the knowledge, there arose the understanding, there arose the wisdom, there arose the light.

21. "So long, O Bhikkhus, as my knowledge and insight were not quite clear, regarding each of these four noble truths in this triple order, in this twelvefold manner—so long was I uncertain whether I had attained to the full insight of that wisdom which is unsurpassed in the heavens or on earth, among the whole race of Samanas and brahmins, or of gods or men.

22. "But as soon, O Bhikkhus, as my knowledge and insight were quite clear regarding each of these four noble truths, in this triple order, in this twelvefold manner—then did I become certain that I had attained to the full insight of that wisdom which is unsurpassed in the heavens or on earth, among the whole race of Samanas and brahmins, or of gods or men.

23. "And now this knowledge and this insight has arisen within me. Immovable is the emancipation of my heart. This is my last existence. There will now be no rebirth for me!"

24. Thus spake the Blessed One. The company of the five Bhikkhus, glad at heart, exalted the words of the Blessed One. And when the discourse had been uttered, there arose within the venerable Kondanna the eye of truth, spotless, and without a stain, (and he saw that) whatsoever has an origin, in that is also inherent the necessity of coming to an end.

*Source*: In *Buddhist Suttas*. Translated from Pali by T. W. Rhys Davids. Sacred Books of the East, vol. 11. Oxford: Clarendon Press, 1881.

# DOCUMENT 5

*The following text is from the* Adittapariyaya Sutta, *which is in the* Samyutta Nikaya *of the Pali Canon, and is typically called the Fire Sermon. It is one of the best known of the Buddha's sermons, simply and powerfully describing the effects of greed, hatred, and delusion. In the sermon, which was delivered in Gaya, to a group of fire-worshipping ascetics, the Buddha uses the metaphor to implicitly criticize the Vedic practice of fire-sacrifice—the dominant form of religion at the time—and at the same time deliver a powerful message that through meditation and concentration one can put out this consuming fire by cultivating a dispassionate aversion to the sensual pleasures of the world, pleasures that create greed and attachment.*

Then The Blessed One, having dwelt in Uruvela as long as he wished, proceeded on his wanderings in the direction of Gaya Head, accompanied by a great congregation of priests, a thousand in number, who had all of them aforetime been monks with matted hair. And there in Gaya, on Gaya Head, The Blessed One dwelt, together with the thousand priests.

And there The Blessed One addressed the priests: "All things, O priests, are on fire. And what, O priests, are all these things which are on fire?

"The eye, O priests, is on fire; forms are on fire; eye-consciousness is on fire; impressions received by the eye are on fire; and whatever sensation, pleasant, unpleasant, or indifferent, originates in dependence on impressions received by the eye, that also is on fire.

"And with what are these on fire?

"With the fire of passion, say I, with the fire of hatred, with the fire of infatuation; with birth, old age, death, sorrow, lamentation, misery, grief, and despair are they on fire.

"The ear is on fire; sounds are on fire; . . . the nose is on fire; odors are on fire; . . . the tongue is on fire; tastes are on fire; . . . the body is on fire; things tangible are on fire; . . . the mind is on fire; ideas are on fire; . . . mind-consciousness is on fire; impressions received by the mind are on fire; and whatever sensation, pleasant, unpleasant, or indifferent, originates in dependence on impressions received by the mind, that also is on fire.

"And with what are these on fire?

"With the fire of passion, say I, with the fire of hatred, with the fire of infatuation; with birth, old age, death, sorrow, lamentation, misery, grief, and despair are they on fire.

"Perceiving this, O priests, the learned and noble disciple conceives an aversion for the eye, conceives an aversion for forms, conceives an aversion for eye-consciousness, conceives an aversion for the impressions received by the eye; and whatever sensation, pleasant, unpleasant, or indifferent, originates in dependence on impressions received by the eye, for that also he conceives an aversion. Conceives an aversion for the ear, conceives an aversion for sounds, . . . conceives an aversion for the nose, conceives an aversion for odors, . . . conceives an aversion for the tongue, conceives an aversion for tastes, . . . conceives an aversion for the body, conceives an aversion for things tangible, . . . conceives an aversion for the mind, conceives an aversion for ideas, conceives an aversion for mind-consciousness, conceives an aversion for the impressions received by the mind; and whatever sensation, pleasant, unpleasant, or indifferent, originates in dependence on impressions received by the mind, for this also he conceives an aversion. And in conceiving this aversion, he becomes divested of passion, and by the absence of passion he becomes free, and when he is free he becomes aware that he is free; and he knows that rebirth is exhausted, that he, has lived the holy life, that he has done what it behooved him to do, and that he is no more for this world."

Now while this exposition was being delivered, the minds of the thousand priests became free from attachment and delivered from the depravities.

*Source:* Henry Clarke Warren. *Buddhism in Translations.* Harvard Oriental Series, vol. 3. Cambridge, MA: Harvard University Press, 1896, 351–353.

## DOCUMENT 6

*The* Dhammapada *is a short canonical Pali text, which consists of 423 verses grouped into 26 chapters. Most of the verses in the text come from other sources. The text seems to have been intended as a kind of catechism, since it could easily have been learned by heart, and presents a basic overview of the Buddha's sayings, addressing fundamental issues such as, in this passage, thirst, or grasping. It continues to be one of the most popular of all Buddhist texts.*

## CHAPTER XXIV: THIRST

334. The thirst of a thoughtless man grows like a creeper; he runs from life to life, like a monkey seeking fruit in the forest.

335. Whomsoever this fierce thirst overcomes, full of poison, in this world, his sufferings increase like the abounding Birana grass.

336. He who overcomes this fierce thirst, difficult to be conquered in this world, sufferings fall off from him, like water-drops from a lotus leaf.

337. This salutary word I tell you, "Do ye, as many as are here assembled, dig up the root of thirst, as he who wants the sweet-scented Usira root must dig up the Birana grass, that Mâaa (the tempter) may not crush you again and again, as the stream crushes the reeds."

338. As a tree, even though it has been cut down, is firm so long as its root is safe, and grows again, thus, unless the feeders of thirst are destroyed, the pain (of life) will return again and again.

339. He whose thirst running towards pleasure is exceeding strong in the thirty-six channels, the waves will carry away that misguided man, viz. his desires which are set on passion.

340. The channels run everywhere, the creeper (of passion) stands sprouting; if you see the creeper springing up, cut its root by means of knowledge.

341. A creature's pleasures are extravagant and luxurious; sunk in lust and looking for pleasure, men undergo (again and again) birth and decay.

342. Men, driven on by thirst, run about like a snared hare; held in fetters and bonds, they undergo pain for a long time, again and again.

343. Men, driven on by thirst, run about like a snared hare; let therefore the mendicant drive out thirst, by striving after passionlessness for himself.

344. He who having got rid of the forest (of lust) (i.e. after having reached Nirvana) gives himself over to forest-life (i.e. to lust), and who, when removed from the forest (i.e. from lust), runs to the forest (i.e. to lust), look at that man! though free, he runs into bondage.

345. Wise people do not call that a strong fetter which is made of iron, wood, or hemp; far stronger is the care for precious stones and rings, for sons and a wife.

346. That fetter wise people call strong which drags down, yields, but is difficult to undo; after having cut this at last, people leave the world, free from cares, and leaving desires and pleasures behind.

347. Those who are slaves to passions, run down with the stream (of

desires), as a spider runs down the web which he has made himself; when they have cut this, at last, wise people leave the world free from cares, leaving all affection behind.

348. Give up what is before, give up what is behind, give up what is in the middle, when thou goest to the other shore of existence; if thy mind is altogether free, thou wilt not again enter into birth and decay.

349. If a man is tossed about by doubts, full of strong passions, and yearning only for what is delightful, his thirst will grow more and more, and he will indeed make his fetters strong.

350. If a man delights in quieting doubts, and, always reflecting, dwells on what is not delightful (the impurity of the body, &c.), he certainly will remove, nay, he will cut the fetter of Mâra.

351. He who has reached the consummation, who does not tremble, who is without thirst and without sin, he has broken all the thorns of life: this will be his last body.

352. He who is without thirst and without affection, who understands the words and their interpretation, who knows the order of letters (those which are before and which are after), he has received his last body, he is called the great sage, the great man.

353. "I have conquered all, I know all, in all conditions of life I am free from taint; I have left all, and through the destruction of thirst I am free; having learnt myself, whom shall I teach?"

354. The gift of the law exceeds all gifts; the sweetness of the law exceeds all sweetness; the delight in the law exceeds all delights; the extinction of thirst overcomes all pain.

355. Pleasures destroy the foolish, if they look not for the other shore; the foolish by his thirst for pleasures destroys himself, as if he were his own enemy.

356. The fields are damaged by weeds, mankind is damaged by passion: therefore a gift bestowed on the passionless brings great reward.

357. The fields are damaged by weeds, mankind is damaged by hatred: therefore a gift bestowed on those who do not hate brings great reward.

358. The fields are damaged by weeds, mankind is damaged by vanity: therefore a gift bestowed on those who are free from vanity brings great reward.

359. The fields are damaged by weeds, mankind is damaged by lust: therefore a gift bestowed on those who are free from lust brings great reward.

*Source: The Dhammapada.* Translated by F. Max Müller. Sacred Books of the East, vol. 10. Oxford: Clarendon Press, 1881, 80–84.

# DOCUMENT 7

*This is a passage from the* Dhammapada, *a short canonical Pali text, which consists of 423 verses grouped into 26 chapters. The text seems to have been intended as a kind of catechism, since it could easily have been learned by heart, and presents a basic overview of the Buddha's sayings, addressing fundamental issues such as, in the prior passage, thirst, or grasping. It continues to be one of the most popular of all Buddhist texts. This passage describes the characteristics that a monk, or bhikkhu, should embody, as the embodiment of a person following the Buddha's teachings.*

## CHAPTER XXV: THE BHIKSHU (MENDICANT)

360. Restraint in the eye is good, good is restraint in the ear, in the nose restraint is good, good is restraint in the tongue.

361. In the body restraint is good, good is restraint in speech, in thought restraint is good, good is restraint in all things. A Bhikshu, restrained in all things, is freed from all pain.

362. He who controls his hand, he who controls his feet, he who controls his speech, he who is well controlled, he who delights inwardly, who is collected, who is solitary and content, him they call Bhikshu.

363. The Bhikshu who controls his mouth, who speaks wisely and calmly, who teaches the meaning and the law, his word is sweet.

364. He who dwells in the law, delights in the law, meditates on the law, follows the law, that Bhikshu will never fall away from the true law.

365. Let him not despise what he has received, nor ever envy others: a mendicant who envies others does not obtain peace of mind.

366. A Bhikshu who, though he receives little, does not despise what he has received, even the gods will praise him, if his life is pure, and if he is not slothful.

367. He who never identifies himself with name and form, and does not grieve over what is no more, he indeed is called a Bhikshu.

368. The Bhikshu who acts with kindness, who is calm in the doctrine of Buddha, will reach the quiet place (Nirvâna), cessation of natural desires, and happiness.

369. O Bhikshu, empty this boat! if emptied, it will go quickly; having cut off passion and hatred thou wilt go to Nirvâna.

370. Cut off the five (senses), leave the five, rise above the five. A Bhikshu, who has escaped from the five fetters, he is called Oghatinna, "saved from the flood."

371. Meditate, O Bhikshu, and be not heedless! Do not direct thy thought to what gives pleasure that thou mayest not for thy heedlessness have to swallow the iron ball (in hell), and that thou mayest not cry out when burning, "This is pain."

372. Without knowledge there is no meditation, without meditation there is no knowledge: he who has knowledge and meditation is near unto Nirvâna.

373. A Bhikshu who has entered his empty house, and whose mind is tranquil, feels a more than human delight when he sees the law clearly.

374. As soon as he has considered the origin and destruction of the elements (khandha) of the body, he finds happiness and joy which belong to those who know the immortal (Nirvâna).

375. And this is the beginning here for a wise Bhikshu: watchfulness over the senses, contentedness, restraint under the law; keep noble friends whose life is pure, and who are not slothful.

376. Let him live in charity, let him be perfect in his duties; then in the fulness of delight he will make an end of suffering.

377. As the Vassika plant sheds its withered flowers, men should shed passion and hatred, O ye Bhikshus!

378. The Bhikshu whose body and tongue and mind are quieted, who is collected, and has rejected the baits of the world, he is called quiet.

379. Rouse thyself by thyself, examine thyself by thyself, thus self-protected and attentive wilt thou live happily, O Bhikshu!

380. For self is the lord of self, self is the refuge of self; therefore curb thyself as the merchant curbs a good horse.

381. The Bhikshu, full of delight, who is calm in the doctrine of Buddha will reach the quiet place (Nirvâna), cessation of natural desires, and happiness.

382. He who, even as a young Bhikshu, applies himself to the doctrine of Buddha, brightens up this world, like the moon when free from clouds.

*Source: The Dhammapada.* Translated by F. Max Müller. Sacred Books of the East, vol. 10. Oxford: Clarendon Press, 1881, 86–88.

# DOCUMENT 8

*The following passage outlines one of the most fundamental monastic rituals in Buddhism, the regular voluntary admission of any transgression in front of the entire* sangha. *This is called the* patimokkha (pratimoksha *in Sanskrit), and is intended to foster discipline and order in the community of monks and to demonstrate to the laity—upon whom the monks are dependent for their physical sustenance—that the monastery is pure. The outward discipline of the monk is intended to be a reflection of his or her inner discipline; the abandonment of worldly possessions and responsibilities is a reflection of his or her detachment, and the serious and sober demeanor a reflection of his or her concentration on enlightenment. The admission of transgressions must be voluntary, since the monk must individually decide to let go, to renounce, any attachment to the transgression.*

Now at that time The Buddha, The Blessed One, was dwelling at Rajagaha on Vulture Peak. And at that time the heretical sect of wandering ascetics met together on the fourteenth, fifteenth, and eighth day of the half-month, and recited their doctrine. And the people drew near to listen to their doctrine, and conceived a liking for the heretical sect of wandering ascetics, and put faith in their teachings; and the heretical sect of wandering ascetics gained adherents.

Now it happened to Seniya Bimbisara, king of Magadha, being in seclusion and plunged in meditation, that a consideration presented itself to his mind, as follows:

"Here the heretical sect of wandering ascetics meet together on the fourteenth, fifteenth, and eighth day of the half-month, and recite their doctrine. And the people draw near to listen to their doctrine, and conceive a liking for the heretical sect of wandering ascetics, and put faith in them; and the heretical sect of wandering ascetics gain adherents. What if now the reverend ones also were to meet together on the fourteenth, fifteenth, and eighth day of the half-month."

Then drew near Seniya Bimbisara, king of Magadha, to where The Blessed One was; and having drawn near and greeted The Blessed One, he sat down respectfully at one side. And seated respectfully at one side, Seniya Bimbisara, king of Magadha, spoke to The Blessed One as follows:

"Reverend Sir, it happened to me, as I was just now seated in seclusion and plunged in meditation, that a consideration presented itself to my mind, as follows: 'Here the heretical sect of wandering ascetics meet together on the fourteenth, fifteenth, and eighth day of the half-month, and recite their doctrine. And the people draw near to listen to their doctrine, and conceive a liking for the heretical sect of wandering ascetics, and put faith in them; and the heretical sect of wandering ascetics gain adherents. What if now the reverend ones also were to meet together on the fourteenth, fifteenth, and eighth day of the half-month?'"

Then The Blessed One enlightened, incited, quickened, and gladdened Seniya Bimbisara, king of Magadha, with a doctrinal discourse. And Seniya Bimbisara, king of Magadha, enlightened, incited, quickened, and gladdened by The Blessed One with a doctrinal discourse, rose from his seat and saluted The Blessed One; and keeping his right side toward him, he departed.

Then The Blessed One, on this occasion and in this connection, after he had delivered a doctrinal discourse, addressed the priests: "I prescribe, O priests, that ye meet together on the fourteenth, fifteenth, and eighth day of the half-month."

Now at that time the priests, having understood that The Blessed One had prescribed that they should meet together on the fourteenth, fifteenth, and eighth day of the half-month, met together on the fourteenth, fifteenth, and eighth day of the half-month, and sat in silence. And the people drew near to listen to the Doctrine, and were angered, annoyed, and spoke indignantly:

"How is it, pray, that the Sakyaputta monks, when they meet together on the fourteenth, fifteenth, and eighth day of the half-month, sit in silence like dumb hogs? Why should they meet together, if not to recite the Doctrine?"

And the priests heard that the people were angered, annoyed, and spoke indignantly. And the priests announced the matter to The Blessed One.

Then The Blessed One, on this occasion and in this connection, after he had delivered a doctrinal discourse, addressed the priests:

"I prescribe, O priests, that when ye have met together on the fourteenth, fifteenth, and eighth day of the half-month, ye recite the Doctrine."

Now it happened to The Blessed One, being in seclusion and plunged in meditation, that a consideration presented itself to his mind, as follows:

"What if now I prescribe that the priests recite a confession [*patimokkha*] of all those precepts which have been laid down by me; and this shall be for them a fast-day duty?"

Then The Blessed One, in the evening of the day, rose from his meditation, and on this occasion and in this connection, after he had delivered a doctrinal discourse, addressed the priests:

"O priests, it happened to me, as I was just now seated in seclusion and plunged in meditation, that a consideration presented itself to my mind, as follows: "What if now I prescribe that the priests recite a confession of all those precepts which have been laid down by me; and this shall be for them a fast-day duty?" I prescribe, O priests, that ye recite a confession. And after this manner, O priests, is it to be recited:

"Let a learned and competent priest make announcement to the congregation, saying, 'Let the reverend congregation hear me. To-day is the fast-day of the fifteenth day of the half-month. If the congregation be ready, let the congregation keep fast-day, and recite the confession. What is the first business before the congregation? Venerable sirs, the proclaiming of your innocency. I will recite the confession and let as many of us as are here present listen carefully and pay strict attention. If anyone have sinned, let him reveal the fact; if he have not sinned, let him remain silent; by your silence I shall know that your reverences are innocent. But now, in assemblages like this, proclamation is made up to the third time, and each one must make confession as if individually asked. But if, when proclamation up to the third time has been made, any priest shall remember a sin and not reveal it, it will be a conscious falsehood. But a conscious falsehood, reverend sirs, has been declared by The Blessed One to be a deadly sin. Therefore, if a priest remember having committed a sin, and desire again to be pure, let him reveal the sin he committed, and when it has been revealed, it shall be well for him.'"

*Source*: Henry Clarke Warren. *Buddhism in Translations*. Harvard Oriental Series, vol. 3. Cambridge, MA: Harvard University Press, 1896, 402–405. Translated from the *Mahavagga* of the *Vinayapitaka* of the Pali Canon.

# DOCUMENT 9

*The status of women in early Buddhism is a matter of much debate. On one hand, there is nothing in the teachings of the Buddha that theoretically indicates that women are in any way inferior to men in terms of their ability to understand and apply the dharma. As the Buddha says to his faithful disciple Ananda, shortly before he dies, the dharma is all that one needs to attain enlightenment, and progress toward that goal is purely a matter of self-effort. However, Buddhism arose in a distinctly patriarchal—and some would say misogynistic—society, in which women were viewed as essentially inferior to men. In the following passage, Ananda petitions the Buddha, on behalf of Maha Pajapati Gotami, the Buddha's aunt, to allow women to join the sangha. The Buddha eventually relents, but stipulates that women must follow an additional eight monastic rules, and, further, that the life of the dharma will be shortened as a result of women being admitted into the order of monks. Although the extra monastic rules may be interpreted as an attempt to insure the sexual purity of the monasteries, the last part is difficult to justify.*

## THE ADMISSION OF WOMEN TO THE ORDER

At that time The Buddha, The Blessed One, was dwelling among the Sakkas at Kapilavatthu in Banyan Park. Then drew near Maha-Pajapati the Gotamid to where The Blessed One was; and having drawn near and greeted The Blessed One, she stood respectfully at one side. And standing respectfully at one side, Maha-Pajapati the Gotamid spoke to The Blessed One as follows:

"Pray, Reverend Sir, let women retire from household life to the houseless one, under the Doctrine and Discipline announced by The Tathagata."

"Enough, O Gotamid, do not ask that women retire from household life to the houseless one, under the Doctrine and Discipline announced by The Tathagata."

And a second time . . . a third . . .

Then thought Maha-Pajapati the Gotamid, "The Blessed One permitteth not that women retire from household life to the houseless one, under the Doctrine and Discipline announced by The Tathagata"; and she was sorrowful, sad, and tearful, and wept. And saluting The Blessed One, and keeping her right side toward him, she departed. . . .

Then Maha-Pajapati the Gotamid had her hair cut off, put on yellow garments, and with a number of Sakka women departed towards Vesali and going from place to place, she drew near to where Vesali was, and Great Wood, and Pagoda Hall. And Maha-Pajapati the Gotamid with swollen feet, and covered with dust, sorrowful, sad, and tearful, stood weeping outside in the entrance porch.

Now the venerable Ananda saw Maha-Pajapati the Gotamid. . . . And he spoke to Maha-Pajapati the Gotamid as follows:

"Wherefore dost thou, O Gotamid, with swollen feet, and covered with dust, sorrowful, sad, and tearful, stand weeping outside in the entrance porch?"

"Because, alas! O Ananda, reverend sir, The Blessed One permitteth not that women retire from household life to the houseless one, under the Doctrine and Discipline announced by The Tathagata."

"In that case, O Gotamid, stay thou here a moment, and I will beseech The Blessed One that women retire from household life to the houseless one, under the Doctrine and Discipline announced by The Tathagata."

Then the venerable Ananda drew near to where The Blessed One was; and having drawn near and greeted The Blessed One, he sat down respectfully at one side. And seated respectfully at one side, the venerable Ananda spoke to The Blessed One as follows:

"Reverend Sir, here this Maha-Pajapati the Gotamid with swollen feet, and covered with dust, sorrowful, sad, and tearful, stands weeping outside in the entrance porch, and says that The Blessed One permitteth not that women retire from household life to the houseless one, under the Doctrine and Discipline announced by The Tathagata. Pray, Reverend Sir, let women retire from household life to the houseless one, under the Doctrine and Discipline announced by The Tathagata."

"Enough, Ananda, do not ask that women retire from household life to the houseless one, under the Doctrine and Discipline announced by The Tathagata."

And a second time . . . a third time. . . .

Then thought the venerable Ananda, "The Blessed One permitteth not that women retire from household life to the houseless one, under the Doctrine and Discipline announced by The Tathagata; what if now, by another route, I beseech The Blessed One that women retire from household life to the houseless one, under the Doctrine and Discipline announced by The Tathagata?"

Then the venerable Ananda spoke to The Blessed One as follows:

"Are women competent, Reverend Sir, if they retire from household life to the houseless one, under the Doctrine and Discipline announced by The Tathagata, to attain to the fruit of conversion, to attain to the fruit of once returning, to attain to the fruit of never returning, to attain to saintship?"

"Women are competent, Ananda, if they retire from household life to the houseless one, under the Doctrine and Discipline announced by The Tathagata, to attain to the fruit of conversion, to attain to the fruit of once returning, to attain to the fruit of never returning, to attain to saintship."

"Since, then, Reverend Sir, women are competent, if they retire from household life to the houseless one, under the Doctrine and Discipline announced by The Tathagata, to attain to the fruit of conversion, to attain to the fruit of once returning, to attain to the fruit of never returning, to attain to saintship, consider, Reverend Sir, how great a benefactress Maha-Pajapati the Gotamid has been. She is the sister of the mother of The Blessed One, and as foster-mother, nurse, and giver of milk, she suckled The Blessed One on the death of his mother. Pray, Reverend Sir, let women retire from household life to the houseless one, under the Doctrine and Discipline announced by The Tathagata."

"If, Ananda, Maha-Pajapati the Gotamid will accept eight weighty regulations, let it be reckoned to her as her ordination:—

"A priestess of even a hundred years' standing shall salute, rise to meet, entreat humbly, and perform all respectful offices for a priest, even if he be but that day ordained. This regulation shall be honored, esteemed, revered, and worshiped, and is not to be transgressed as long as life shall last.

"A priestess shall not keep residence in a district where there are no priests. This regulation shall be honored, esteemed, revered, and worshiped, and is not to be transgressed as long as life shall last.

"On each half-month a priestess shall await from the congregation of the priests the appointing of fast-day, and some one to come and administer the admonition. This regulation shall be honored, esteemed, revered, and worshiped, and is not to be transgressed as long as life shall last.

"At the end of residence a priestess shall invite criticism in both congregations in regard to what has been seen, or heard, or suspected. This regulation shall be honored, esteemed, revered, and worshiped, and is not to be transgressed as long as life shall last.

"If a priestess be guilty of serious sin, she shall undergo penance of half a month toward both the congregations. This regulation shall be honored, esteemed, revered, and worshiped, and is not to be transgressed as long as life shall last.

"When a female novice has spent her two years in the practice of the six rules, she shall seek ordination from both the congregations. This regulation shall be honored, esteemed, revered, and worshiped, and is not to be transgressed as long as life shall last.

"A priestess shall not revile or abuse a priest in any manner. This regulation shall be honored, esteemed, revered, and worshiped, and is not to be transgressed as long as life shall last.

"From this day on the priestesses shall not be allowed to reprove the priests officially, but the priests shall be allowed to reprove the priestesses officially. This regulation shall be honored, esteemed, revered, and worshiped, and is not to be transgressed as long as life shall last.

"If, Ananda, Maha-Pajapati the Gotamid will accept these eight weighty regulations, let it be reckoned to her as her ordination."

"If, Ananda, women had not retired from household life to the houseless one, under the Doctrine and Discipline announced by The Tathagata, religion, Ananda, would long endure; a thousand years would the Good Doctrine abide. But since, Ananda, women have now retired from household life to the houseless one, under the Doctrine and Discipline announced by The Tathagata, not long, Ananda, will religion endure; but five hundred years, Ananda, will the Good Doctrine abide. Just as, Ananda, those families which consist of many women and few men are easily overcome by burglars, in exactly the same way, Ananda, when women retire from household life to the houseless one, under a doctrine and discipline, that religion does not long endure. Just as, Ananda, when the disease called mildew falls upon a flourishing field of rice, that field of rice does not long endure, in exactly the same way, Ananda, when women retire from household life to the houseless one, under a doctrine and discipline, that religion does not long endure. Even as, Ananda, when the disease called rust falls upon a flourishing field of sugar-cane, that field of sugar-cane does not long endure, in exactly the same way, Ananda, when women retire from household life to the houseless one, under a doctrine and discipline, that religion does not long endure. And just as, Ananda, to a large pond a man would prudently build a dike, in order that the water might not transgress its bounds, in exactly the same way, Ananda, have I prudently laid down eight weighty regulations, not to be transgressed as long as life shall last."

*Source:* Henry Clarke Warren. *Buddhism in Translations.* Harvard Oriental Series, vol. 3. Cambridge, MA: Harvard University Press, 1896, 441–447. Translated from the *Cullavagga* of the *Vinayapitaka* of the Pali Canon.

# DOCUMENT 10

*The* Mahaparinibbana Sutta, *which appears in the* Digha Nikaya *of the Pali Tipitaka, narrates the last days and death of the Buddha. It is notable for many things, including a long discussion about what to do with the Buddha's relics after he is dead. The passage quoted here narrates the scene just after Ananda, the Buddha's faithful disciple, has learned that his teacher and companion is soon to pass out of existence. The talk the Buddha delivers to Ananda emphasizes that the teachings the Buddha has left behind, the* dharma, *are to be the monks' guide in the future, equivalent to the Buddha himself.*

Then The Blessed One addressed the priests:

"Where, O priests, is Ananda?"

"Reverend Sir, the venerable Ananda has entered the monastery, and leaning against the bolt of the door, he weeps, saying, 'Behold, I am but a learner, and not yet perfect, and my Teacher is on the point of passing into Nirvana, he who was so compassionate to me.'" Then The Blessed One addressed a certain priest, saying,—

"Go, O priest, and say to the venerable Ananda from me, 'The Teacher calleth thee, brother Ananda.'"

"Yes, Reverend Sir," said the priest to The Blessed One in assent, and drew near to where the venerable Ananda was; and having drawn near, he spoke to the venerable Ananda as follows:—

"The Teacher calleth thee, brother Ananda."

"Yes, brother," said the venerable Ananda to the priest in assent, and drew near to where The Blessed One was; and having drawn near and greeted The Blessed One, he sat down respectfully at one side. And the venerable Ananda being seated respectfully at one side, The Blessed One spoke to him as follows:—

"Enough, Ananda, do not grieve, nor weep. Have I not already told you, Ananda, that it is in the very nature of all things near and dear unto us that we must divide ourselves from them, leave them, sever ourselves from them? How is it possible, Ananda, that whatever has been born, has come into being, is organized and perishable, should not perish? That condition is not possible. For a long time, Ananda, have you waited on The Tathagata with a kind, devoted, cheerful, single-hearted, unstinted service of body, with a kind, devoted, cheerful, single-hearted, unstinted service of voice, with a kind, devoted, cheerful, single-hearted, unstinted service of mind. You have acquired much merit, Ananda; exert yourself, and soon will you be free from all depravity."

Then The Blessed One addressed the priests:—

"Priests, of all those Blessed Ones who aforetime were saints and Supreme Buddhas, all had their favorite body-servants, just as I have now my Ananda. And, priests, of all those Blessed Ones who in the future shall be saints and Supreme Buddhas, all will have their favorite body-servants, just as I have now my Ananda. Wise, O priests, is Ananda—he knows when it is a fit time to draw near to see The Tathagata, whether for the priests, for the priestesses, for the lay disciples, for the female lay disciples, for the king, for the king's courtiers, for the leaders of heretical sects, or for their adherents.

"Ananda, O priests, has four wonderful and marvelous qualities. And what are the four? O priests, if an assembly of priests draw near to behold Ananda, it is delighted with beholding him; and if then Ananda hold a discourse on the Doctrine, it is also delighted with the discourse; and when Ananda, O priests, ceases to speak, the assembly of priests is still unsated. O priests, if an assembly of priestesses . . . an assembly of lay disciples . . . an assembly of female lay disciples draw near to behold Ananda, it is delighted with beholding him; and if then Ananda hold a discourse on the Doctrine, it is also delighted with the discourse; and when Ananda, O priests, ceases to speak, the assembly of female lay disciples is still unsated. . . ."

Then The Blessed One addressed the venerable Ananda:—

"It may be, Ananda, that some of you will think, 'The word of The Teacher is a thing of the past; we have now no Teacher.' But that, Ananda, is not the correct view. The Doctrine and Discipline, Ananda, which I have taught and enjoined upon you is to be your teacher when I am gone. But whereas now, Ananda, all the priests address each other with the title of 'brother,' not so must they address each other after I am gone. A senior priest, Ananda, is to address a junior priest either by his given name, or by his family name, or by the title of 'brother'; a junior priest is to address a senior priest with the title 'reverend sir,' or 'venerable.' . . ."

Then The Blessed One addressed the priests:—

"It may be, O priests, that some priest has a doubt or perplexity respecting either The Buddha or the Doctrine or the Order or the Path or the course of conduct. Ask any questions, O priests, and suffer not that afterwards ye feel remorse, saying, 'Our Teacher was present with us, but we failed to ask him all our questions.'"

When he had so spoken, the priests remained silent.

And a second time The Blessed One, and a third time The Blessed One addressed the priests:—

"It may be, O priests, that some priest has a doubt or perplexity respecting either The Buddha or the Doctrine or the Order or the Path or the course of conduct. Ask any question, O priests, and suffer not that afterwards ye feel remorse, saying, 'Our Teacher was present with us, but we failed to ask him all our questions.'"

And a third time the priests remained silent.

Then The Blessed One addressed the priests:—

"It may be, O priests, that it is out of respect to The Teacher that ye ask no questions. Then let each one speak to his friend."

And when he had thus spoken, the priests remained silent.

Then the venerable Ananda spoke to The Blessed One as follows:—

"It is wonderful, Reverend Sir! It is marvellous, Reverend Sir! Reverend Sir, I have faith to believe that in this congregation of priests not a single priest has a doubt or perplexity respecting either The Buddha or the Doctrine or the Order or the Path or the course of conduct."

"With you, Ananda, it is a matter of faith, when you say that; but with The Tathagata, Ananda, it is a matter of knowledge that in this congregation of priests not a single priest has a doubt or perplexity respecting either The Buddha or the Doctrine or the Order or the Path or the course of conduct. For of all these five hundred priests, Ananda, the most backward one has become converted, and is not liable to pass into a lower state of existence, but is destined necessarily to attain supreme wisdom."

Then The Blessed One addressed the priests:—

"And now, O priests, I take my leave of you; all the constituents of being are transitory; work out your salvation with diligence."

And this was the last word of The Tathagata.

*Source*: Henry Clarke Warren. *Buddhism in Translations*. Harvard Oriental Series, vol. 3. Cambridge, MA: Harvard University Press, 1896, 98–110.

# DOCUMENT 11

*One of the hallmarks of Buddhist doctrinal literature is the intense philosophical analysis that Buddhist authors engage in. Part of this stems from the basic idea in Buddhism that all things are interdependent, that they have a cause—as classically articulated in the* paticcasamuppada *(pratityasamutpada in Sanskrit) formula—and thus are devoid of any ultimate reality. In the* Abhidamma *literature of the Pali Canon, the workings of* karma *particularly receive a great deal of analytical attention. In the following passage, the great Theravada commentator Buddhaghosa addresses the issue of* karma, *discussing in a clear and concise manner the various types of* karma. *His overarching point here is that all* karma—*positive and negative—ultimately have ignorance as their cause.*

The kinds of karma are those already briefly mentioned, as consisting of the triplet beginning with meritorious karma and the triplet beginning with bodily karma, making six in all.

To give them here in full, however, meritorious karma consists of the eight meritorious thoughts which belong to the realm of sensual pleasure and show themselves in alms-giving, keeping the precepts, etc., and of the five meritorious thoughts which belong to the realm of form and show themselves in ecstatic meditation,—making thirteen thoughts; demeritorious karma consists of the twelve demeritorious thoughts which show themselves in the taking of life etc.; and karma leading to immovability consists of the four meritorious thoughts which belong to the realm of formlessness and show themselves in ecstatic meditation. Accordingly these three karmas consist of twenty-nine thoughts.

As regards the other three, bodily karma consists of the thoughts of the body, vocal karma of the thoughts of the voice, mental karma of the thoughts of the mind. The object of this triplet is to show the avenues by which meritorious karma etc. show themselves at the moment of the initiation of karma.

For bodily karma consists of an even score of thoughts, namely, of the eight meritorious thoughts which belong to the realm of sensual pleasure and of the twelve demeritorious ones. These by exciting gestures show themselves through the avenue of the body.

Vocal karma is when these same thoughts by exciting speech show themselves through the avenue of the voice. The thoughts, however, which belong to the realm of form, are not included, as they do not form a dependence for subsequent consciousness. And the case is the same with the thoughts which belong to the realm of formlessness. Therefore they also are to be excluded from the dependence of consciousness. However, all depend on ignorance.

Mental karma, however, consists of all the twenty-nine thoughts, when they spring up in the mind without exciting either gesture or speech.

Thus, when it is said that ignorance is the dependence of the karma-triplet consisting of meritorious karma etc., it is to be understood that the other triplet is also included.

But it may be asked, "How can we tell that these karmas are dependent on ignorance?" Because they exist when ignorance exists.

For, when a person has not abandoned the want of knowledge concerning misery etc., which is called ignorance, then by that want of knowledge concerning misery and concerning anteriority etc. he seizes on the misery of the round of rebirth with the idea that it is happiness and hence begins to perform the threefold karma which is its cause; by that want of knowledge concerning the origin of misery and by being under the impression that thus happiness is secured, he begins to perform karma that ministers to desire, though such karma is really the cause of misery; and by that want of knowledge concerning cessation and the path and under the impression that some particular form of existence will prove to be the cessation of misery, although it really is not so, or that sacrifices, alarming the gods by the greatness of his austerities, and other like procedures are the way to cessation, although they are not such a way, he begins to perform the threefold karma.

Moreover, through this non-abandonment of ignorance in respect of the Four Truths, he does not know the fruition of meritorious karma to be the misery it really is, seeing that it is completely overwhelmed with the calamities, birth, old age, disease, death, etc.; and so to obtain it he begins to perform meritorious karma in its three divisions of bodily, vocal, and mental karma, just as a man in love with a heavenly nymph will throw himself down a precipice. When he does not perceive that at the end of that meritorious fruition considered to be such happiness comes the agonizing misery of change and disappointment, he begins to perform the meritorious karma above described, just as a locust will fly into the flame of a lamp, or a man that is greedy after honey will lick the honey-smeared edge of a knife. When he fails to perceive the calamities due to sensual gratification and its fruition, and, being under the impression that sensuality is happiness, lives enthralled by his passions, he then begins to perform demeritorious karma through the three avenues, just as a child will play with filth, or one who wishes to die will eat poison. When he does not perceive the misery of the change that takes place in the constituents of being, even in the realm of formlessness, but has a perverse belief in persistence etc., he begins to perform mental karma that leads to immovability, just as a man who has lost his way will go after a mirage.

As, therefore, karma exists when ignorance exists but not when it does not exist, it is to be understood that this karma depends on ignorance. And it has been said as follows:

"O priests, the ignorant, uninstructed man performs meritorious karma, demeritorious karma, and karma leading to immovability. But whenever, O priests, he abandons his ignorance and acquires wisdom, he through the fading out of ignorance and the coming into being of wisdom does not even perform meritorious karma."

*Source*: Henry Clarke Warren. *Buddhism in Translations*. Harvard Oriental Series, vol. 3. Cambridge, MA: Harvard University Press, 1896, 298–300. Translated from Chapter 6 of Buddhaghosa's *Visuddhimagga* (The Path of Purity).

## DOCUMENT 12

*The* Milindapanha *(Questions of King Milinda) is one of the most important noncanonical Pali texts. It records a lengthy dialogue between a Buddhist monk named Nagasena and the Greek king Milinda. Milinda poses a series of questions to Nagasena that address what appear to be contradictions in Buddhist doctrine, and Nagasena gives clear, concise answers, marked by similes and analogies that make even the most complex of Buddhist doctrines accessible. In the following passage, which contains one of the most well known similes in all of Buddhism, Milinda questions Nagasena about the concept of* anatta, *or no self.*

Now Milinda the king went up to where the venerable Nagasena was, and addressed him with the greetings and compliments of friendship and courtesy, and took his seat respectfully apart. And Nagasena reciprocated his courtesy, so that the heart of the king was propitiated.

And Milinda began by asking, "How is your Reverence known, and what, Sir, is your name?"

"I am known as Nagasena, O king, and it is by that name that my brethren in the faith address me. But although parents, O king, give such a name as Nagasena, or Surasena, or Virasena, or Sihasena, yet this, Sire,— Nagasena and so on—is only a generally understood term, a designation in common use. For there is no permanent individuality (no soul) involved in the matter."

Then Milinda called upon the Yonakas and the brethren to witness: "This Nagasena says there is no permanent individuality (no soul) implied in his name. Is it now even possible to approve him in that?" And turning to Nagasena, he said: "If, most reverend Nagasena, there be no permanent individuality (no soul) involved in the matter, who is it, pray, who gives to you members of the Order your robes and food and lodging and necessaries for the sick? Who is it who enjoys such things when given? Who is it who lives a life of righteousness? Who is it who devotes himself to meditation? Who is it who attains to the goal of the Excellent Way, to the Nirvana of Arahatship? And who is it who destroys living creatures? who is it who takes what is not his own? who is it who lives an evil life of worldly lusts, who speaks lies, who drinks strong drink, who (in a word) commits any one of the five sins which work out their bitter fruit even in this life? If that be so there is neither merit nor demerit; there is neither doer nor causer of good or evil deeds; there is neither fruit nor result of good or evil Karma. –If, most reverend Nagasena, we are to think that were a man to kill you there would be no murder, then it follows that there are no real masters or teachers in your Order, and that your ordinations are void.–You tell me that your brethren in the Order are in the habit of addressing you as Nagasena. Now what is that Nagasena? Do you mean to say that the hair is Nagasena?"

"I don't say that, great king."

"Or the hairs on the body, perhaps?"

"Certainly not."

"Or is it the nails, the teeth, the skin, the flesh, the nerves, the bones, the marrow, the kidneys, the heart, the liver, the abdomen, the spleen, the lungs, the larger intestines, the lower intestines, the stomach, the fæces, the bile, the phlegm, the pus, the blood, the sweat, the fat, the tears, the serum, the saliva, the mucus, the oil that lubricates the joints, the urine, or the brain, or any or all of these, that is Nagasena?"

And to each of these he answered no.

"Is it the outward form then (Rupa) that is Nagasena, or the sensations (Vedana), or the ideas (Sañña), or the confections (the constituent elements of character, Samkhara), or the consciousness (Vigññana), that is Nagasena?"

And to each of these also he answered no.

"Then is it all these Skandhas combined that are Nagasena?"

"No! great king."

"But is there anything outside the five Skandhas that is Nagasena?"

And still he answered no.

"Then thus, ask as I may, I can discover no Nagasena. Nagasena is a mere empty sound. Who then is the Nagasena that we see before us? It is a falsehood that your reverence has spoken, an untruth!"

And the venerable Nagasena said to Milinda the king: "You, Sire, have been brought up in great luxury, as beseems your noble birth. If you were to walk this dry weather on the hot and sandy ground, trampling under foot the gritty, gravelly grains of the hard sand, your feet would hurt you. And as your body would be in pain, your mind would be disturbed, and you would experience a sense of bodily suffering. How then did you come, on foot, or in a chariot?"

"I did not come, Sir, on foot. I came in a carriage."

"Then if you came, Sire, in a carriage, explain to me what that is. Is it the pole that is the chariot?"

"I did not say that."

"Is it the axle that is the chariot?"

"Certainly not."

"Is it the wheels, or the framework, or the ropes, or the yoke, or the spokes of the wheels, or the goad, that are the chariot?"

And to all these he still answered no.

"Then is it all these parts of it that are the chariot?"

"No, Sir."

"But is there anything outside them that is the chariot?"

And still he answered no.

"Then thus, ask as I may, I can discover no chariot. Chariot is a mere empty sound. What then is the chariot you say you came in? It is a falsehood that your Majesty has spoken, an untruth! There is no such thing as a chariot! You are king over all India, a mighty monarch. Of whom then are you afraid that you speak untruth? And he called upon the Yonakas and the brethren to witness, saying: "Milinda the king here has said that he came by carriage. But when asked in that case to explain what the carriage was, he is unable to establish what he averred. Is it, forsooth, possible to approve him in that?"

When he had thus spoken the five hundred Yonakas shouted their applause, and said to the king: "Now let your Majesty get out of that if you can?"

And Milinda the king replied to Nagasena, and said: "I have spoken no untruth, reverend Sir. It is on account of its having all these things—the pole, and the axle, the wheels, and the framework, the ropes, the yoke, the spokes, and the goad—that it comes under the generally understood term, the designation in common use, of 'chariot.'"

"Very good! Your Majesty has rightly grasped the meaning of 'chariot.' And just even so it is on account of all those things you questioned me about—the thirty-two kinds of organic matter in a human body, and the five constituent elements of being—that I come under the generally understood term, the designation in common use, of 'Nagasena.' For it was said, Sire, by our Sister Vagira in the presence of the Blessed One:

"Just as it is by the condition precedent of the co-existence of its various parts that the word 'chariot' is used, just so is it that when the Skandhas are there we talk of a 'being.'"

"Most wonderful, Nagasena, and most strange. Well has the puzzle put to you, most difficult though it was, been solved. Were the Buddha himself here he would approve your answer. Well done, well done, Nagasena!"

*Source: The Questions of King Milinda.* Translated by T. W. Rhys Davids. Sacred Books of the East, vol. 35. Oxford: Oxford University Press, 1890, 40–45.


# DOCUMENT 13

*The* Visuddhimagga, *which translates literally as "the path of purification," is a vast compendium of Theravada Buddhist philosophy, meditation, and commentary on the Buddha's teachings. It remains one of the most important and authoritative texts in the Theravada Buddhist world. Written by the great monk and scholar Buddhaghosa in the fifth century* C.E., *in Sri Lanka, the* Visuddhimagga *outlines, in meticulous detail, the path to nirvana. At times, Buddhaghosa writes with graphic detail, particularly when describing the human body; there are long passages in the text outlining funeral-ground meditation, which involves a monk meditating on a rotting body in order to fully understand the impermanence of the physical self. In the following passage, Buddhaghosa takes a somewhat less morbid, but no less graphic tack in his analysis of the body.*

For as the body when dead is repulsive, so is it also when alive; but on account of the concealment afforded by an adventitious adornment, its repulsiveness escapes notice. The body is in reality a collection of over three hundred bones, and is framed into a whole by means of one hundred and eighty joints. It is held together by nine hundred tendons, and overlaid by nine hundred muscles, and has an outside envelope of moist cuticle covered by an epidermis full of pores, through which there is an incessant oozing and trickling, as if from a kettle of fat. It is a prey to vermin, the seat of disease, and subject to all manner of miseries. Through its nine apertures it is always discharging matter, like a ripe boil. Matter is secreted from the two eyes, wax from the ears, snot from the nostrils, and from the mouth issue food, bile, phlegm, and blood, and from the two lower orifices of the body faeces and urine, while from the ninety-nine thousand pores of the skin an unclean sweat exudes attracting black flies and other insects.

Were even a king in triumphal progress to neglect the use of tooth-sticks, mouth-rinses, anointings of the head, baths and inner and outside garments, and other means for beautifying the person, he would become as uncouth and unkempt as the moment he was born, and would in no wise differ in bodily offensiveness from the low-caste candâla whose occupation it is to remove dead flowers. Thus in respect of its uncleanness, malodor, and disgusting offensiveness, the person of a king does not differ from that of a candâla. However, when, with the help of tooth-sticks, mouth-rinses, and various ablutions, men have cleansed their teeth, and the rest of their persons, and with manifold garments have covered their nakedness, and have anointed themselves with many-colored and fragrant unguents, and adorned themselves with flowers and ornaments, they find themselves able to believe in an "I" and a "mine." Accordingly, it is on account of the concealment afforded by this adventitious adornment that people fail to recognize the essential repulsiveness of their bodies, and that men find pleasure in women, and women in men. In reality, however, there is not the smallest just reason for being pleased.

A proof of this is the fact that when any part of the body becomes detached, as, for instance, the hair of the head, hair of the body, nails, teeth, phlegm, snot, faeces, or urine, people are unwilling so much as to touch it, and are distressed at, ashamed of, and loathe it. But in respect of what remains, though that is likewise repulsive, yet men are so wrapped in blindness and infatuated by a passionate fondness for their own selves, that they believe it to be something desirable, lovely, lasting, pleasant, and an Ego.

In this they resemble the old jackal of the forest, who supposes each flower on a kimsuka tree to be a piece of meat, until disconcerted by its falling from the tree.

Therefore,

> *Even as the jackal, when he sees*
> *The flowers on a kimsuka tree,*
> *Will hasten on, and vainly think,*
> *"Lo, I have found a tree with meat!"*
>
> *But when each several flower that falls*
> *He bites with an exceeding greed,*
> *"Not this is meat; that one is meat*
> *Which in the tree remains," he says;*
>
> *Even so the sage rejects and loathes*
> *Each fallen particle as vile,*
> *But thinks the same of all the rest*
> *Which in the body still remain.*
>
> *Yet fools the body pleasant find,*
> *Become therewith infatuate,*
> *And many evil works they do,*
> *Nor find from misery their release.*
>
> *Let, then, the wise reflect, and see*
> *The body is of grace bereft;*
> *Whether it living be or dead,*
> *Its nature is putridity.*
>
> *For it has been said,*
>
> *"The body, loathsome and unclean,*
> *Is carrion-like, resembles dung,*
> *Despised by those whose eyes can see,*
> *Though fools find in it their delight.*
>
> *"This monstrous wound hath outlets nine,*
> *A damp, wet skin doth clothe it o'er;*
> *At every point the filthy thing*
> *Exudeth nasty, stinking smells.*

*"If now this body stood revealed,*
*Were it but once turned inside out,*
*We sure should need to use a stick*
*To keep away the dogs and crows."*

Therefore the undisciplined priest must acquire the mental reflex wherever he can, wherever an impurity appears, be it in a living body or in one that is dead, and thus bring his meditation to the stage of attainment-concentration.

*Source*: Henry Clarke Warren. *Buddhism in Translations*. Harvard Oriental Series, vol. 3. Cambridge, MA: Harvard University Press, 1896, 298–300. Translated from Chapter 6 of Buddhaghosa's *Visuddhimagga* (The Path of Purity).

# DOCUMENT 14

*Among the earliest of Mahayana Buddhist texts are the* Perfection of Wisdom, *or* Prajnaparapmita, Sutras, *which were probably composed beginning in about 100* B.C.E. *Some of these texts were extremely long— up to 100,000 verses—making them extremely difficult to memorize, transcribe, and transport. The* Hrdaya Sutra, *or* Heart Sutra, *is the shortest and perhaps also the most popular sutra in Mahayana Buddhism. It summarizes, in an extremely condensed form, the fundamental teaching of the larger* Perfection of Wisdom *texts. In particular, the* Heart Sutra *expresses the early Mahayana emphasis on the emptiness, or* shunyata, *of all things.*

Adoration to the Omniscient!

This I heard: At one time the Bhagavat dwelt at Ragagriha, on the hill Gridhrakuta, together with a large number of Bhikshus and a large number of Bodhisattvas.

At that time the Bhagavat was absorbed in a meditation, called Gambhiravasambodha. And at the same time the great Bodhisattva Aryavalokitesvara, performing his study in the deep Prajnaparamita, thought thus: "There are the five Skandhas, and those he (the Buddha?) considered as something by nature empty."

Then the venerable Shariputra, through Buddha's power, thus spoke to the Bodhisattva Aryavalokitesvara: "If the son or daughter of a family wishes to perform the study in the deep Prajnaparamita, how is he to be taught?"

On this the great Bodhisattva Aryavalokitesvara thus spoke to the venerable Shariputra: "If the son or daughter of a family wishes to perform the study in the deep Prajnaparamita, he must think thus:

"There are five Skandhas, and these he considered as by their nature empty. Form is emptiness, and emptiness indeed is form. Emptiness is not different from form, form is not different from emptiness. What is form that is emptiness, what is emptiness that is form. Thus perception, name, conception, and knowledge also are emptiness. Thus, O Shariputra, all things have the character of emptiness, they have no beginning, no end, they are faultless and not faultless, they are not imperfect and not perfect. Therefore, O Shariputra, here in this emptiness there is no form, no perception, no name, no concept, no knowledge. No eye, ear, nose, tongue, body, and mind. No form, sound, smell, taste, touch, and objects. There is no eye," &c., till we come to "there is no mind, no objects, no mind-knowledge. There is no knowledge, no ignorance, no destruction (of ignorance)," till we come to "there is no decay and death, no destruction of decay and death; there are not (the Four Truths, viz.) that there is pain, origin of pain, stoppage of pain, and the path to it. There is no knowledge, no obtaining, no not-obtaining of Nirvana. Therefore, O Shariputra, as there is no obtaining (of Nirvana), a man who has approached the Prajnaparamita of the Bodhisattvas, dwells (for a time) enveloped in consciousness. But when the envelopment of consciousness has been annihilated, then he becomes free of all fear, beyond the reach of change, enjoying final Nirvana.

"All Buddhas of the past, present, and future, after approaching the Prajnaparamita, have awoke to the highest perfect knowledge.

"Therefore we ought to know the great verse of the Prajnaparamita, the verse of the great wisdom, the unsurpassed verse, the verse which appeases all pain—it is truth, because it is not false—the verse proclaimed in the Prajnaparamita: 'O wisdom, gone, gone, gone to the other shore, landed at the other shore, Svaha!'

"Thus, O Sariputra, should a Bodhisattva teach in the study of the deep Prajnaparamita."

Then when the Bhagavat had risen from that meditation, he gave his approval to the venerable Bodhisattva Avalokitesvara, saying: "Well done, well done, noble son! So it is, noble son. So indeed must this study of the deep Prajnaparamita be performed. As it has been described by thee, it is applauded by Arhat Tathagatas." Thus spoke Bhagavat with joyful mind. And the venerable Sariputra, and the honourable Bodhisattva Avalokitesvara, and the whole assembly, and the world of gods, men, demons, and fairies praised the speech of the Bhagavat.

Here ends the Prajnaparamitahridayasutra.

*Source: The Heart Sutra (Hrdaya Sutra), in Buddhist Mahayana Texts.* Translated by E. B. Cowell, F. Max Müller, and J. Takakusu. Sacred Books of the East, vol. 49. Oxford: Clarendon Press, 1894, 147–149.

# DOCUMENT 15

*Like the* Heart Sutra, *the* Diamond Sutra (Vajracchedika Sutra) *is a condensed version of the much longer* Pefection of Wisdom (Prajnaparamita) *texts that were among the earliest and the most important Mahayana Buddhist texts produced in India beginning in about 100* B.C.E. *The* Diamond Sutra *was extremely popular in early Mahayana Buddhism—and continues to be today—no doubt due to its brevity and clarity of doctrine. Whereas the emphasis in the much shorter* Heart Sutra *is almost solely placed on the central Mahayana doctrine of emptiness* (shunyata), *the* Diamond Sutra *is somewhat more expansive in its discussion of doctrine. In the passages that follow, a particular characteristic of many early Mahayana texts is emphasized: the degree to which the text celebrates itself as the foremost expression of the Buddha's* dharma, *to the point that anyone who copies, writes, or hears the* sutra *gains more merit than virtually any other activity. Indeed, the text should be revered in the same way that a* chaitya—*a repository containing the physical relics of the Buddha—should be treated.*

## III

Then the Bhagavat thus spoke to him: "Any one, O Subhuti, who has entered here on the path of the Bodhisattvas must thus frame his thought: As many beings as there are in this world of beings, comprehended under the term of beings (either born of eggs, or from the womb, or from moisture, or miraculously), with form or without form, with name or without name, or neither with nor without name, as far as any known world of beings is known, all these must be delivered by me in the perfect world of Nirvana. And yet, after I have thus delivered immeasurable beings, not one single being has been delivered. And why? If, O Subhuti, a Bodhisattva had any idea of (belief in) a being, he could not be called a Bodhisattva (one who is fit to become a Buddha). And why? Because, O Subhuti, no one is to be called a Bodhisattva, for whom there should exist the idea of a being, the idea of a living being, or the idea of a person."

## VIII

Bhagavat said: "What do you think, O Subhuti, if a son or daughter of a good family filled this sphere of a million millions of worlds with the seven gems or treasures, and gave it as a gift to the holy and enlightened Tathagatas, would that son or daughter of a good family on the strength of this produce a large stock of merit?" Subhuti said: "Yes, O Bhagavat, yes, O Sugata, that son or daughter of a good family would on the strength of this produce a large stock of merit. And why? Because, O Bhagavat, what was preached by the Tathagata as the stock of merit, that was preached by the Tathagata as no-stock of merit. Therefore the Tathagata preaches: 'A stock of merit, a stock of merit indeed!'" Bhagavat said: "And if, O Subhuti, the son or daughter of a good family should fill this sphere of a million millions of worlds with the seven treasures and should give it as a gift to the holy and enlightened Tathagatas, and if another after taking from this treatise of the Law one Gatha of four lines only should fully teach others and explain it, he indeed would on the strength of this produce a larger stock of merit immeasurable and innumerable. And why? Because, O Subhuti, the highest perfect knowledge of the holy and enlightened Tathagatas is produced from it; the blessed Buddhas are produced from it. . . . "

## XI

Bhagavat said: "What do you think, O Subhuti, if there were as many Ganga rivers as there are grains of sand in the large river Ganga, would the grains of sand be many?" Subhuti said: "Those Ganga rivers would indeed be many, much more the grains of sand in those Ganga rivers."

Bhagavat said: "I tell you, O Subhuti, I announce to you, If a woman or man were to fill with the seven treasures as many worlds as there would be grains of sand in those Ganga rivers and present them as a gift to the holy and fully enlightened Tathagatas—What do you think, O Subhuti, would that woman or man on the strength of this produce a large stock of merit?" Subhuti said: "Yes, O Bhagavat, yes, O Sugata, that woman or man would on the strength of this produce a large stock of merit, immeasurable and innumerable." Bhagavat said: "And if, O Subhuti, a woman or man having filled so many worlds with the seven treasures should give them as a gift to the holy and enlightened Tathagatas, and if another son or daughter of a good family, after taking from this treatise of the Law one Gatha of four lines only, should fully teach others and explain it, he, indeed, would on the strength of this produce a larger stock of merit, immeasurable and innumerable."

## XII

"Then again, O Subhuti, that part of the world in which, after taking from this treatise of the Law one Gatha of four lines only, it should be preached or explained, would be like a Chaitya (holy shrine) for the whole world of gods, men, and spirits; what should we say then of those who learn the whole of this treatise of the Law to the end, who repeat it, understand it, and fully explain it to others? They, O Subhuti, will be endowed with the highest wonder. And in that place, O Subhuti, there dwells the teacher, or one after another holding the place of the wise preceptor."

## XV

"And if, O Subhuti, a woman or man sacrificed in the morning as many lives as there are grains of sand in the river Ganga and did the same at noon and the same in the evening, and if in this way they sacrificed their lives for a hundred thousands of niyutas of kotis of ages, and if another, after hearing this treatise of the Law, should not oppose it, then the latter would on the strength of this produce a larger stock of merit, immeasurable and innumerable. What should we say then of him who after having written it, learns it, remembers it, understands it, and fully explains it to others?

"And again, O Subhuti, this treatise of the Law is incomprehensible and incomparable. And this treatise of the Law has been preached by the Tathagata for the benefit of those beings who entered on the foremost path (the path that leads to Nirvana), and who entered on the best path. And those who will learn this treatise of the Law, who will remember it, recite it, understand it, and fully explain it to others, they are known, O Subhuti, by the Tathagata through his Buddha-knowledge, they are seen, O Subhuti, by the Tathagata through his Buddha-eye. All these beings, O Subhuti, will be endowed with an immeasurable stock of merit, they will be endowed with an incomprehensible, incomparable, immeasurable and unmeasured stock of merit. All these beings, O Subhuti, will equally remember the Bodhi (the highest Buddha-knowledge), will recite it, and understand it. And why? Because it is not possible, O Subhuti, that this treatise of the Law should be heard by beings of little faith, by those who believe in self, in beings, in living beings, and in persons. It is impossible that this treatise of the Law should be heard by beings who have not acquired the knowledge of Bodhisattvas, or that it should be learned, remembered, recited, and understood by them. The thing is impossible.

"And again, O Subhuti, that part of the world in which this Sutra will be propounded, will have to be honoured by the whole world of gods, men, and evil spirits, will have to be worshipped, and will become like a Chaitya (a holy sepulchre)."

*Source: The Vajracchedika*, in *Buddhist Mahayana Texts*. Translated by E. B. Cowell, F. Max Müller, and J. Takakusu. Sacred Books of the East, vol. 49. Oxford: Clarendon Press, 1894.

# DOCUMENT 16

*One of the central concepts of early Mahayana Buddhism is the principle of skillful means, or upaya. According to the doctrine of upaya, the Buddha and the bodhisattvas, out of their selfless compassion to save all beings from samsara, use any means possible to enlighten beings, including, if necessary, telling a lie. In the following passage, taken from the Lotus Sutra, one of the most influential of all Mahayana texts, the metaphor of the "burning house," one of the most famous metaphors in all of Mahayana Buddhism, is used to explain the need for skillful means.*

## CHAPTER 3

Let us suppose the following case, Sariputra. In a certain village, town, borough, province, kingdom, or capital, there was a certain housekeeper, old, aged, decrepit, very advanced in years, rich, wealthy, opulent; he had a great house, high, spacious, built a long time ago and old, inhabited by some two, three, four, or five hundred living beings. The house had but one door, and a thatch; its terraces were tottering, the bases of its pillars rotten, the coverings and plaster of the walls loose. On a sudden the whole house was from every side put in conflagration by a mass of fire. Let us suppose that the man had many little boys, say five, or ten, or even twenty, and that he himself had come out of the house.

Now, Sariputra, that man, on seeing the house from every side wrapt in a blaze by a great mass of fire, got afraid, frightened, anxious in his mind, and made the following reflection: I myself am able to come out from the burning house through the door, quickly and safely, without being touched or scorched by that great mass of fire; but my children, those young boys, are staying in the burning house, playing, amusing, and diverting themselves with all sorts of sports. They do not perceive, nor know, nor understand, nor mind that the house is on fire, and do not get afraid. Though scorched by that great mass of fire, and affected with such a mass of pain, they do not mind the pain, nor do they conceive the idea of escaping.

The man, Sariputra, is strong, has powerful arms, and (so) he makes this reflection: I am strong, and have powerful arms; why, let me gather all my little boys and take them to my breast to effect their escape from the house. A second reflection then presented itself to his mind: This house has but one opening; the door is shut; and those boys, fickle, unsteady, and childlike as they are, will, it is to be feared, run hither and thither, and come to grief and disaster in this mass of fire. Therefore I will warn them. So resolved, he calls to the boys: Come, my children; the house is burning with a mass of fire; come, lest ye be burnt in that mass of fire, and come to grief and disaster. But the ignorant boys do not heed the words of him who is their well-wisher; they are not afraid, not alarmed, and feel no misgiving; they do not care, nor fly, nor even know nor understand the purport of the word "burning"; on the contrary, they run hither and thither, walk about, and repeatedly look at their father; all, because they are so ignorant.

Then the man is going to reflect thus: The house is burning, is blazing by a mass of fire. It is to be feared that myself as well as my children will come to grief and disaster. Let me therefore by some skilful means get the boys out of the house. The man knows the disposition of the boys, and has a clear perception of their inclinations. Now these boys happen to have many and manifold toys to play with, pretty, nice, pleasant, dear, amusing, and precious. The man, knowing the disposition of the boys, says to them: My children, your toys, which are so pretty, precious, and admirable, which you are so loth to miss, which are so various and multi-farious, (such as) bullock-carts, goat-carts, deer-carts, which are so pretty, nice, dear, and precious to you, have all been put by me outside the house-door for you to play with. Come, run out, leave the house; to each of you I shall give what he wants. Come soon; come out for the sake of these toys. And the boys, on hearing the names mentioned of such playthings as they like and desire, so agreeable to their taste, so pretty, dear, and de-lightful, quickly rush out from the burning house, with eager effort and great alacrity, one having no time to wait for the other, and pushing each other on with the cry of "Who shall arrive first, the very first?"

The man, seeing that his children have safely and happily escaped, and knowing that they are free from danger, goes and sits down in the open air on the square of the village, his heart filled with joy and delight, released from trouble and hindrance, quite at ease. The boys go up to the place where their father is sitting, and say: "Father, give us those toys to play with, those bullock-carts, goat-carts, and deer-carts." Then, Sariputra, the man gives to his sons, who run swift as the wind, bullock-carts only, made of seven precious substances, provided with benches, hung with a multitude of small bells, lofty, adorned with rare and wonderful jewels, embellished with jewel wreaths, decorated with garlands of flowers, car-peted with cotton mattresses and woollen coverlets, covered with white cloth and silk, having on both sides rosy cushions, yoked with white, very fair and fleet bullocks, led by a multitude of men. To each of his children he gives several bullock-carts of one appearance and one kind, provided with flags, and swift as the wind. That man does so, Sariputra, because be-ing rich, wealthy, and in possession of many treasures and granaries, he rightly thinks: Why should I give these boys inferior carts, all these boys being my own children, dear and precious? I have got such great vehicles, and ought to treat all the boys equally and without partiality. As I own many treasures and granaries, I could give such great vehicles to all beings, how much more then to my own children. Meanwhile the boys are mounting the vehicles with feelings of astonishment and wonder. Now, Sariputra, what is thy opinion? Has that man made himself guilty of a falsehood by first holding out to his children the prospect of three vehicles and afterwards giving to each of them the greatest vehicles only, the most magnificent vehicles?

Sariputra answered: By no means, Lord; by no means, Sugata. That is not sufficient, O Lord, to qualify the man as a speaker of falsehood, since it only was a skilful device to persuade his children to go out of the burning house and save their lives. Nay, besides recovering their very body, O Lord, they have received all those toys. If that man, O Lord, had given no single cart, even then he would not have been a speaker of falsehood, for he had previously been meditating on saving the little boys from a great mass of pain by some able device. Even in this case, O Lord, the man would not have been guilty of falsehood, and far less now that he, considering his having plenty of treasures and prompted by no other motive but the love of his children, gives to all, to coax them, vehicles of one kind, and those the greatest vehicles. That man, Lord, is not guilty of falsehood.

*Source: The Saddharma-Pundarika, or The Lotus of the True Law.* Translated by H. Kern. Sacred Books of the East, vol. 21. Oxford: Oxford University Press, 1884.

# GLOSSARY OF
# SELECTED TERMS

**Abhidhamma (Skt., abhidharma):** Scholastic and philosophical analysis and elaboration on the Buddha's teachings; one of the three main divisions of the Buddhist Canon.

**Anatta (Skt., anatman):** No self; the idea that there is no permanent, unchanging, essential essence to personhood.

**Anicca (Skt., anitya):** The doctrine of impermanence; one of the three characteristics of existence (with *dukkha* and *anatta*).

**Arahant (Skt., arhat):** A Buddhist saint; one who has attained enlightenment.

**Bhikkhu, Bhikkhuni (Skt., bhikshu, bhikshuni):** A monk, nun.

**Bodhi tree:** The tree under which Siddhartha Gautama attained enlightenment.

**Bodhisattva (Pali, bodhisatta):** The Buddha before he attained enlightenment; in the Mahayana, an enlightened being.

**Cakravartin (Pali, cakkavattin):** Literally, a "wheel turner," a great king who rules according to the Buddha's teachings.

**Dana:** The practice of giving, which accumulates merit.

**Dharma (Pali, dhamma):** The teachings of the Buddha, the "truth," or "law." Also, in philosophical discussions, a basic element of reality.

**Dukkha:** "Suffering," unsatisfactoriness, the first of the noble truths.

**Eightfold Path:** The religious path articulated by the Buddha in his first sermon, consisting of Right Understanding, Right Thinking, Right Speech, Right Attitude, Right Livelihood, Right Effort, Right Mindfulness, and Right Concentration.

**Four Noble Truths:** One of the most basic distillations of the Buddha's teachings; they are (1) suffering (*dukkha*) exists in the world; (2) suffering arises, or has a cause (*samudaya*); (3) suffering has an end (*nirodha*); and (4) there is a path, the Eightfold Path, that leads to enlightenment (*magga*).

**Gautama (sometimes Gotama):** The family name of the historical Buddha.

**Hinayana:** Literally, the "lesser vehicle," the Mahayana term for what becomes known as the Theravada school of Buddhism, one of the two main divisions of Buddhism; also called "southern Buddhism."

**Jataka:** A story concerning one of the prior lives of the Buddha.

**Karma (Pali, kamma):** Literally, "action"; the basic law of cause and effect, by which actions produce lasting results.

**Karuna:** Compassion.

**Khandha (Skt., skandha):** One of the "five aggregates" that engender clinging; a basic element of personality.

**Lotus Sutra:** *Saddharmapundarika Sutra*, an important early Mahayana scripture.

**Mahayana:** Literally, the "greater vehicle," also sometimes referred to as "northern Buddhism," one of the two main schools of Buddhism.

**Maitreya (Pali, Meteyya):** The Buddha-to-be, an important savior bodhisattva in the Mahayana.

**Manjushri:** A principal savior bodhisattva in the Mahayana.

**Mara:** The embodiment of lust and desire, a being who tests the Buddha's
enlightenment.

**Nikaya:** A section of the Pali Canon; also a school of Buddhism.

**Nirodha:** Literally, "cessation," the third noble truth.

**Nirvana (Pali, nibbana):** Absolute extinction of suffering and its causes.

**Parinirvana (Pali, parinibbana):** The end of the Buddha's physical existence (i.e., his death).

**Paticcasamuppada (Skt., pratityasamutpada):** Interdependent origination; the Buddhist doctrine of causality.

**Pattimokkha (Skt., pratimoksha):** The list of rules that govern monastic
life, recited formally once every two weeks by the assembled monks.

**Pratyekabuddha (Pali, paccekabuddha):** A "solitary awakened one," an
enlightened being who, unlike the Buddha, does not share the insights that led to enlightenment.

**Precepts:** A basic set of standards for ethical conduct.

**Rains retreat:** The period, especially in early, premonastic Buddhism,
during the monsoons (usually three months) when monks and nuns
gathered and resided in one place, devoting themselves to study and
practice.

**Samadhi:** Meditative concentration.

**Samsara:** The cycle of birth, life, death, and rebirth, characterized by suffering (*dukkha*), in which all living beings are caught.

**Sangha:** The Buddhist community, especially the monks and nuns.

**Shakyamuni:** Literally, "sage of the Shakya clan," a common epithet of the historical Buddha.

**Shila:** Morality or ethics.

**Shramana:** A wanderer, one who has abandoned the householder's life and set out in search of enlightenment.

**Shravaka:** A disciple, one who hears the Buddha's teachings; in the Mahayana, a follower of the Hinayana.

**Siddhartha (Pali, Siddhatta):** The personal name of the Buddha.

**Sutra (Pali, sutta):** A doctrinal discourse attributed to the Buddha; one of the principal divisions of the Buddhist Canon.

**Tathagata:** Literally, the "thus-gone one," an epithet of the Buddha.

**Theravada:** The "way of the elders," also called "southern Buddhism," or "Hinayana" (by the Mahayana), one of the principal divisions of Buddhism.

**Tripitaka (Pali, Tipitaka):** The "three baskets" of Buddhist scripture; the Buddhist Canon, consisting of the *Vinaya*, *Sutra*, and *Abhidharma* texts.

**Triple Gem:** The Buddha, *dharma*, and the *sangha*.

**Vajrayana:** Sometimes translated as the "thunderbolt" or "diamond" vehicle; a development of Mahayana Buddhism, sometimes called the "third turning," most prominent in Tibet.

**Vinaya:** The monastic code of discipline.

**Zen (also Ch'an):** A school of Mahayana Buddhism that began in China and took root in Japan.

# ANNOTATED
# BIBLIOGRAPHY

## BOOKS

Ashvaghosha. *Buddhacarita; or, Acts of the Buddha*. Edited by E. H. Johnston. New Delhi: Motilal Banarsidass, 1984. One of the earliest full biographies of the Buddha, written by the first-century Indian Buddhist Ashvaghosha. Contains a wealth of stories, myths, doctrine, and general information about the life of the historical Buddha.

Bechert, Heinz, and Richard Gombrich, eds. *The World of Buddhism: Monks and Nuns in Society and Culture*. London: Thames and Hudson, 1984. Contains many excellent illustrations of Buddhist art and practice, with articles covering a wide array of topics from a range of Buddhist scholars.

Blackstone, Kathryn R. *Women in the Footsteps of the Buddha: Struggles for Liberation in the Therigatha*. London: Curzon, 1998. A clear, well-presented treatment of women in early Buddhism, with a specific focus on the Pali text *Therigatha*. Analyses the verses in this important early text and explores the differences in attitudes toward secular social roles and the experience of liberation of the female and male authors of these texts.

Cabezon, Jose Ignacia, ed. *Buddhism, Sexuality, and Gender*. Albany: SUNY Press, 1992. A more advanced set of essays dealing with gender issues, including a section on gay issues in Buddhism. Very useful in putting some more contemporary issues into the context of early Buddhism.

Carrithers, Michael. *The Buddha*. Oxford: Oxford University Press, 1983. A remarkably concise yet exceedingly clear treatment of the Buddha's life story.

Carter, John Ross, and Malinda Palihawadana, trans. *The Dhammapada*. New York: Oxford University Press, 1987. Contains extensive material from the commentaries and alternative versions of the *Dhammapada* preserved by other schools. A fundamental early text that is still in wide use throughout the Buddhist world.

Ch'en, Kenneth K. S. *The Chinese Transformation of Buddhism*. Princeton, NJ: Princeton University Press, 1973. A very useful overview of the importation of Buddhism into China and the major changes that the Buddhist tradition underwent in China.

Conze, Edward. *Buddhist Texts through the Ages*. New York: Harper Torchbooks, 1964. A very useful collection of translations of texts from several different schools.

————. *Buddhist Thought in India*. Ann Arbor: University of Michigan Press, 1967. A solid and mostly reliable survey of Indian Buddhist thought.

————, ed. *The Perfection of Wisdom in Eight Thousand Lines and Its Verse Summary* [*Ashtasahasrika Prajnaparamita Sutra*]. Bolinas, CA: Four Seasons Foundation, 1973. One of the most important early Mahayana Buddhist texts. A clear translation with a useful introduction.

Coomaraswamy, Ananda K. *Elements of Buddhist Iconography*. Cambridge, MA: Harvard University Press, 1935. A dated but nonetheless important early interpretation of symbolism in Buddhist art, which argues against the idea that Buddhists got the idea to represent the Buddha from the Greeks.

Cowel, E. B., ed. *Buddhist Mahayana Texts*. New York: Dover, 1989. A well-balanced collection of translations of a variety of Mahayana texts.

Crosby, Kate, and A. Skilton, trans. *The Bodhicaryavatara*. New York: Oxford University Press, 1995. A very important fifth-century Indian Buddhism text, written by Shantideva, that lays out the path of the bodhisattva and establishes a kind of foundation for proper Mahayana practice. A clear translation.

Dallapiccola, Anna, ed. *The Stupa: Its Religious, Historical, and Architectural Significance*. Wiesbaden: Franz Steiner Verlag, 1980. A very detailed discussion of one of the most important physical structures in Buddhist life.

De Silva, Padmasiri. *An Introduction to Buddhist Psychology*. London: Macmillan, 1979. A lucid and useful introduction to the complex topic of Buddhist Psychology, dealing with both the early textual traditions and the issues in the contemporary world.

Dehejia, Vidya. *Discourse in Early Buddhist Art: Visual Narratives of India*. New Delhi: Munshiram Manoharlal, 1997. A somewhat controversial presentation of Buddhist art that focuses on the ways in which the early stories of the Buddha's life were told through sculpture. Very useful for understanding the function of art in early Buddhism.

Dumoulin, Heinrich. *Zen Buddhism: A History*. 2 vols. New York: Macmillan, 1988–1990. A clear and comprehensive history of the development and history of Zen.

Dutt, Sukumar. *Buddhist Monks and Monasteries of India*. London: George Allen and Unwin, 1962. An important study on the early *sangha* in India up to the thirteenth century. Includes discussions of sources, doctrinal traditions, and daily life based on the archaeological remains. Contains a particularly useful discussion of the relationship between monastic organization and lay *sanghas*.

Eckel, Malcolm David. *To See the Buddha*. Princeton, NJ: Princeton University Press, 1992. A fascinating philosophical study of what it means to see an image of the Buddha, through the eyes of a medieval Indian Buddhist philosopher. Very technical, but well worth the effort. Helps to put into perspective early Buddha-image practices in ancient India.

Fisher, Robert E. *Buddhist Art and Architecture*. London: Thames and Hudson, 1993. A clear and comprehensive general introduction to the development of Buddhist art and architecture.

Gethin, Rupert. *The Foundations of Buddhism*. New York: Oxford University Press, 1998. A very clear, concise introduction to the basic doctrinal structure of Buddhism.

Gombrich, Richard F. *How Buddhism Began: The Conditioned Genesis of the Early Teachings*. London: Athlone Press, 1996. A collection of lectures on the development of early Buddhism from one of the leading Buddhist scholars in the West. Gombrich uses the early texts of the tradition to expand upon key issues such as *karma* and meditation, and pays close attention to how early doctrinal issues shaped the development of the *sangha* and Buddhism in general.

———. *Theravada Buddhism: A Social History from Ancient Benares to Modern Colombo*. London: Routledge and Kegan Paul, 1988. The early chapters are useful for an overview of India at the time of the Buddha. Later chapters are more concerned with Sri Lanka. Useful in linking ancient Buddhism with the contemporary Buddhist world.

Griffiths, Paul J. *On Being Buddha: The Classical Doctrine of Buddhahood*. Albany: State University of New York Press, 1981. A difficult philosophical text that focuses on the conception of the Buddha and Buddhahood in early and medieval texts. Appropriate for more advanced students.

Harvey, Peter. *An Introduction to Buddhism: Teachings, History and Practices.* Cambridge: Cambridge University Press, 1990. This is a comprehensive introductory book, particularly strong on matters of doctrine.

———. *An Introduction to Buddhist Ethics: Foundations, Values, and Issues.* Cambridge: Cambridge University Press, 2000. A clear and systematic introduction to Buddhists that explores the nature and practice of Buddhist ethics in a variety of contexts, placing the early doctrinal discussions into the context of contemporary issues such as war, abortion, homosexuality, and so on.

Huntington, Susan, and John Huntington. *The Art of Ancient India.* New York: Weatherhill, 1985. A detailed survey of ancient Indian art, with ample attention paid to Buddhism. Over 700 illustrations and clear but very detailed discussions of a wide range of monuments, temples, and individual images. Not just an overview, this book really goes into great depths.

Jayawickrama, N. A., trans. *The Story of Gautama Buddha: The Nidana-katha of the Jatakathakatha.* Oxford: Pali Text Society, 1990. An introduction to the *Jataka* stories written by the important fifth-century Buddhist commentator Buddhaghosa. Provides an excellent introduction to Buddhist commentarial texts, and is an important exposition of the prior lives of the historical Buddha.

Kalupahana, David. *Nagarjuna, the Philosophy of the Middle Way.* New York: State University of New York Press, 1986. A very detailed, important study of Nagarjuna, perhaps the most important philosopher in the early Mahayana tradition.

Karetzky, Patricia E. *The Life of the Buddha: Ancient Scriptural and Pictorial Traditions.* Lanham, MD: University Press of America, 1992. A highly readable overview of the biography of the Buddha as it is played out both in texts and in art.

Keown, Damien. *Buddhist Ethics: A Very Short Introduction.* Oxford: Oxford University Press, 2005. An extremely clear overview of Buddhist ethical discourse. Puts a number of important contemporary issues, from abortion to war, into a Buddhist context.

King, Winston. *Theravada Meditation: The Buddhist Transformation of Yoga.* State Park: Pennsylvania State University Press, 1980. A clear and concise discussion of the basics of Buddhism meditation, taking into account, particularly, the ways in which the Buddha transformed earlier Upanishadic notions of meditation, and also some of the important similarities between Hindu yoga and Buddhist meditation.

Kinnard, Jacob N. *Imaging Wisdom: Seeing and Knowing in the Art of Indian Buddhism*. Surrey: Curzon, 1999. Focuses on ways in which medieval Indian Buddhists visually represented wisdom, or *prajna*. Also discusses the larger issue of the theory and practice of image making and veneration in early Buddhism.

Kitagawa, Joseph Mitsuo, and Mark D. Cummings. *Buddhism and Asian History*. New York: Macmillan, 1989. A comprehensive set of chapters dealing with the historical development of Buddhism in India and other parts of Asia.

Knox, Robert. *Amaravati: Buddhist Sculpture from the Great Stupa*. London: British Museum Press, 1992. Presents recent research on the history of one of the most significant Buddhist monuments in southern India. Insightful analysis, and excellent photos.

Lamotte, Etienne. *History of Indian Buddhism: From the Origins to the Saka Era* (translated from the original French: *Histoire du bouddhisme indien*, 1958). Louvain-La-Neuve: Institut Orientaliste, 1988. Something of a classic in the field of Buddhist studies, this is a clear, authoritative work with a special emphasis on the historical development of Buddhism in India.

Liebert, Gosta. *Iconographical Dictionary of the Indian Religions: Hinduism, Buddhism, Jainism*. Leiden, The Netherlands: Brill, 1976. A very useful book that carefully defines the terms, iconographic forms, and deities of Buddhist art.

Liu, Xinru. *Ancient India and Ancient China: Trade and Religious Exchanges, AD 1–600*. New York: Oxford University Press, 1988. A very interesting study that deals with the role that traders traveling along the ancient highways of India and China played in the spread of Buddhist ideas and practices.

Lopez, Donald S., Jr., ed. *Buddhism in Practice*. Princeton, NJ: Princeton University Press, 1995. A collection of translations of primary texts, which focus on nonelite, "popular" forms of Buddhist belief, ritual, and practice. Includes useful introductions by many prominent scholars.

Mitchell, Donald W. *Buddhism: Introducing the Buddhist Experience*. New York: Oxford University Press, 2002. A good general introduction. Proceeds historically, beginning with the life and teachings of Gautama Buddha, the early Buddhist debates, and ending with contemporary Buddhism both in Asia and in the West. Includes personal narratives from leading Buddhist figures explaining various facets of Buddhist life and practice.

Mitra, Debala. *Buddhist Monuments.* Calcutta, India: Sahitya Samsad, 1971. An excellent description of over sixty important Buddhist sites in India, Pakistan, and southern Nepal. Includes discussions of the development of *stupas*, various architectural monuments, and monasteries.

Murcott, Susan. *The First Buddhist Women.* Berkeley, CA: Parallax Press, 1991. A contemporary feminist analysis of the *Therigatha*, an important early collection of women's religious poetry. Murcott discusses the lives and significance of a variety of figures—wives, mothers, teachers, courtesan, prostitutes, and wanderers—who became central to the emerging Buddhist community.

Nikam, N. A., and R. McKeon, eds. *The Edicts of Ashoka.* Chicago: Univesity of Chicago Press, 1978. Clear translations of Ashoka's major pronouncements on the proper Buddhist mode of living, edicts that were inscribed on pillars throughout India by the great Buddhist king in the fourth century B.C.E. Includes a useful orienting introduction.

Nyanamoli, Bhikkhu, trans. *The Path of Purification; or, Visuddhimagga.* Kandy, Sri Lanka: Buddhist Publication Society, 1991. A very clear translation of Buddhaghosa's work that defines Theravada doctrine in Sri Lanka and Burma, with a fine introduction by the translator.

Nyanamoli, Bhikku, and Bhikkhu Bodhi, trans. *Middle Length Discourses of the Buddha.* Boston: Wisdom Publications, 1995. Clear translation of a very important early text on meditation, the *Middle Length Discourses of the Buddha*, from the *Majjhima Nikaya* of the Pali Canon.

Nyanaponika, Thera. *The Heart of Buddhist Meditation: A Handbook of Mental Training Based on the Buddha's Way of Mindfulness.* Colombo, Sri Lanka: The Word of the Buddha Publishing Committee, 1956. A clear presentation of some of the basics of Buddhist meditation. Focuses primarily on the Vipassana tradition. Includes a short anthology of meditation texts taken from the Theravada (Pali) Canon.

Pal, Pratapaditya. *Light of Asia: Buddha Sakyamuni in Asian Art.* Los Angeles: County Museum of Art, 1984. Excellent reproductions of images of the Buddha from a variety of contexts. Contains useful introductory matter and discussions of individual images.

Rahula, Walpola. *What the Buddha Taught.* New York: Grove Press, 1974. A very popular work, read widely both in the West and in Asia. Presents the basic doctrines of early Buddhist thought in modern rationalist dress. One of the clearest statements of modern scholarly Protestant Buddhism.

Reynolds, Frank E., and Jason A. Carbine, eds. *The Life of Buddhism*. Berkeley: University of California Press, 2000. An insightful set of essays that attempt to highlight key aspects of "lived" Buddhism. Overall, there is an emphasis on the contemporary context, but nearly all of the essays attempt to put the contemporary life of Buddhism into the larger historical development of the tradition. Very good, in particular, on ritual dimensions of Buddhism.

Schober, Juliane, ed. *Sacred Biography in the Buddhist Traditions of South and Southeast Asia*. Honolulu: University of Hawaii Press, 1997. Essays discussing the structure and function of biographical narratives in Indian and Theravadin Buddhist traditions, starting with the narratives of the Buddha's lives, and extending up to narratives of modern Theravadin figures. This is very useful in putting the focus on the Buddha's biography in early Buddhism into a contemporary perspective.

Snellgrove, David L., ed. *The Image of the Buddha*. Tokyo: Kodansha International, 1978. A lavishly illustrated volume, covers the evolution of the Buddha image, and traces its development through the medieval period. Covers a large geographical range as well. Very useful as a detailed overview of the ways in which the Buddha has been depicted and the various contexts in which Buddha images are situated.

———. *Indo-Tibetan Buddhism: Indian Buddhists and Their Tibetan Successors*, 2 vols. Boston: Shambhala, 1987. The first volume presents an overview of Indian Buddhism, while the second consists of a study of Indian Tantrism, together with proto-Tantric elements in earlier Mahayana.

Snelling, John. *The Buddhist Handbook: A Complete Guide to Buddhist Teaching, Practice, History, and Schools*. London: Century, 1987. A useful general resource and reference work.

Strong, John. *The Legend of King Asoka*. Princeton, NJ: Princeton University Press, 1983. A clear translation and discussion of the *Asokavadana*, the Sarvastivadin legend of the fourth-century-B.C.E. king Asoka. Includes complex analysis and historical context.

Swearer, Donald K. *The Buddhist World of Southeast Asia*. Albany: State University of New York Press, 1995. A survey work that focuses on the history and practices of Buddhism in Southeast Asia. Very clear, with a particularly strong emphasis on contemporary practices.

Trainor, Kevin. *Relics, Rituals, and Representation in Buddhism: Rematerializing the Sri Lankan Theravada Tradition*. Cambridge: Cambridge University Press,

1997. A focused study of the development of relic veneration in Buddhism, beginning with the early Pali materials. Although this book focuses on Sri Lanka, it puts it into the context of early Buddhism in India.

Warder, A. K. *Indian Buddhism*. Rev. ed. New Delhi: Motilal Banarsidass, 1980. A good general survey of Indian Buddhism that is especially clear on matters of doctrine and philosophy.

Warren, Henry C. *Buddhism in Translations*. New York: Atheneum, 1963. A comprehensive selection of translation from Pali texts. The language is somewhat dated, but the breadth of the collection makes it very useful.

Wijayaratna, Mohan. *Buddhist Monastic Life According to the Texts of the Theravada Tradition*. Translated by Claude Grangier and Steven Collins. Cambridge: Cambridge University Press, 1990. A very good, very readable general introduction to the topic of *vinaya* and its relation to the *dharma*.

Williams, Paul. *Mahayana Buddhism: The Doctrinal Foundations*. London: Routledge and Kegan Paul, 1989. An excellent survey of the thought and development of the Mahayana.

Williams, Paul, with Anthony Tribe. *Buddhist Thought: A Complete Introduction to the Indian Tradition*. London: Routledge, 2000. A more advanced overview of Mahayana thought and Indian Buddhist history. Clear discussions of the relationship between various Mahayana and non-Mahayana schools of thought in ancient India, specific topics within the Mahayana, and the development of various buddhas and bodhisattvas, up to the rise of the Vajrayana.

Wiltshire, Martin Gerald. *Ascetic Figures before and in Early Buddhism: The Emergence of Gautama as the Buddha*. Berlin: Mouton de Gruyter, 1990. A more advanced study of the various ascetic figures who were contemporaries of the Buddha.

Zwalf, W. *Buddhism: Art and Faith*. London: British Museum Publications, 1985. A useful although somewhat overly general overview of Buddhist art.

## ONLINE RESOURCES

Buddha Dharma Education Association, Inc. www.buddhanet.net/
An excellent general source, containing scholarly articles, bibliographies, short overviews, etc.

Buddhist Dictionary of Pali Proper Names, www.palikanon.com/english/
    pali_names/dic_idx.html
    A very useful dictionary of Pali words and names, helpful in sorting out
various terms and figures.

Buddhist Studies, WWW Virtual Library www.ciolek.com/WWWVL-
    Buddhism.html
    An omnibus site with a wealth of information.

DharmaNet International, www.dharmanet.org
    A comprehensive general source.

Internet Sacred Text Archive, www.sacred-texts.com/bud/index.htm
    Offers translations of a wide range of Buddhist texts.

## FILMS

*Blue Collar and Buddha*, 1988; 57 mins. Available at www.filmakers.com, or
    through Cornell University's Southeast Asia Video Loan Collection/Media
    Services, www.einaudi.cornell.edu/SoutheastAsia/. A documentary that
    explores the dilemma of a community of Laotian refugees, torn between
    preserving their cultural identity and adapting to their new life in Amer-
    ica. Resettling in Rockford, Illinois, they find their working-class neighbors
    resent their economic gains.

*Buddha and the Rice Planters*, 1981; 30 mins. Available through the University of
    Pennsylvania's South Asia Center at http://www.southasiacenter.upenn
    .edu/about.htm. A comprehensive look at popular Buddhist traditions of
    Sri Lanka using a village near Kandy as the locale.

*Buddha on the Silk Road*, 1998; 60 mins. Available through Mystic Fire Videos at
    www.mysticfire.com Follows the path of Xuanzang during his journey from
    China to India in the seventh century. Includes dramatic footage of Bud-
    dhist sites in China, Tibet, and India.

*Buddhism*, 1999; 57 mins. Available through Films for the Humanities and Sci-
    ences, www.films.com. Part of the series "On the Trails of World Reli-
    gions." In this film, the religious scholar Hans Küng narrates a basic
    overview of the Buddhist tradition, beginning with Bodhgaya and ending
    at a Zen Buddhist monastery in Japan, to offer an overview of the many
    branches and traditions in Buddhism today.

*Buddhism*, 2003; 26 mins. Available through Films for the Humanities and Sciences, www.films.com. Part of the series "Heaven on Earth: Monuments to Belief," this film uses architecture and art to examine the birth of Buddhism in India and its spread to other lands. The Mahabodhi Temple in Bodhgaya; the Great Stupa at Sanchi, India; the Borobudur Temple—the largest Buddhist shrine in the world—in Indonesia; and the Chuang Yen Monastery in New York State, with its 37-foot-tall marble statue of The Enlightened One surrounded by 10,000 smaller statues, are featured.

*Buddhism Comes to America*, 1999; 30 mins. Available through the Hartley Film Foundation, www.hartleyvideos.org. Explores the growth of Buddhism in America. The video combines archival material and recent footage of the Living Dharma Center, whose director tells why he and his students were attracted to the Buddha. It also features D. T. Suzuki and Alan Watts.

*Buddhism: Path to Enlightenment*, 1978; 35 mins. Available through the Hartley Film Foundation, www.hartleyvideos.org. Traces the life of the Buddha from his birth as a prince, through time spent as a wandering mendicant in search of a solution to life's sorrows, to his later years when he trudged the dusty paths of India preaching his ego-shattering, life-redeeming message.

*Buddhism: The Great Wheel of Being*, 1999; 52 mins. Available through Films for the Humanities and Sciences, www.films.com. A basic introduction, includes on-location footage from various pilgrimage places in India.

*Buddhism: The Way of Compassion*, 2000; 28 mins. Available through the Social Studies School Service, www.socialstudies.com. Offers a glimpse into monastery life in Thailand and Japan, an overview of various rituals and art forms, and includes interviews with monks Eido Roshi and Jomgon Kontrol Rimpoche.

*Footprint of the Buddha*, 1977; 52 mins. Available through Ambrose Video Publishing, www.ambrosevideo.com. Part of the Long Search series, this video was shot mostly in Sri Lanka, and explores some of the basics of the Buddha's teachings. Includes interviews with monks and lay Buddhists.

*The Four Noble Truths*, 1997; 4 hours. Available through Mystic Fire Videos, www.mysticfire.com. In July 1996, His Holiness the 14th Dalai Lama gave two days of teachings on the Four Noble Truths at the Barbican Hall in London. This video series presents those lectures.

*In the Spirit of Manjushri: The Wisdom Teachings of Buddhism*, 1999; 4 hours. Available through Mystic Fire Videos, www.mysticfire.com. A video-document of three days in May 1998, during which His Holiness the Dalai Lama presented the teachings at Roseland Auditorium in New York City. Includes an introduction and commentary by Robert A. F. Thurman.

*The Life of the Buddha,* 2003; 51 mins. Available through Films for the Humanities and Sciences, www.films.com. Produced by the BBCW, this film dramatizes the life of the Buddha. Various scholars and monks provide commentaries.

*Robert A. F. Thurman on Buddhism: The Buddha-The Dharma-The Sangha,* 1999; 4 hours. Available through Mystic Fire Videos, www.mysticfire.com. Thurman presents a broad overview of the Buddhist tradition, with particular focus on relevance to contemporary Americans.

# INDEX

*Abhidhamma*. See *Abhidharma*
*Abhidharma*, 23, 59, 64, 67, 70,
    81–82, 86, 89, 92–93, 127
Agni, xxii, xxx
Ajivikas, xxxi–xxxii, 29–30
Alara Kalama, 10
Amaravati, 32, 47–48, 51–53, photo
    6
Ambedhkar, B. R., 73
Ananda, 22, 25, 27, 43–44, 50, 55,
    79–80, 117–123, 124–126
*anatman*, 21. See also *anatta*; no self
*anatta*, 129–132. See also *anatman*;
    no self
*Anguttara Nikaya*, 7, 79
aniconic thesis, 48
*Arhats*, 14, 59–60
Arnold, Sir Edwin, 74
Asanga, 80–81, 92
asceticism, xx, xxiii, xxix–xxxi, 6, 8,
    10–13, 15, 17, 27, 29, 35, 41,
    49, 70
Ashoka, 36–39, 52, 81–82, 87; edicts
    of, 38–39, 81; pilgrimage of, 40,
    50–52; and relics of the
    Buddha, 46
*ashtamahapratiharya*, 54

Ashvaghosha, 8–9, 99
*AtharvaVeda*, xxiii
*atman*, 21
*Avadanas*, 64; in art, 48
Avalokiteshvara, 62, 66, 135–137
*avatara*, 71

Bharhut, 48, 52–53, photo section
*bhumisparsha mudra*, 12, 51
Bimbisara, 36, 117
Blavatsky, Helena Petrovna, 74
Bodhgaya, 13, 40, 47–48, 50–51, 73,
    106, photo 4
*bodhi*, 2, 12–13, 140
Bodhi tree, 13, 41, 47, 51, 103, 106
*bodhicitta*, 61
bodhisattvas, 4, 59–61, 66, 69–70,
    72, 135–140; Buddha as, 5,
    98–99
Bodies of the Buddha. See *kayas*
Brahman, xxii, xxix–xxxi
*Brahmanas*, xxii
Brahmanism, xix
brahmin, xxii–xxiii, xxvi, xxxi
*Brhad Aranyaka Upanishad*, xxix
Buddha, "historical," 2; names of, 5
*buddha anusmrti*, 50

*Buddhacarita*, 8–9, 99, 103, 106
Buddhaghosa, 82–83, 127, 132, 135
*buddha puja*, 49
Buddhas, prior and future, 2
*buddhata*, 63
*buddhavacana*, 57, 64
*Buddhist Catechism*, 74
burning house, 140–143

*cakravartin* (*cakkavattin*), 5, 10, 36
caste, xxv–vi
Ch'an. *See* Zen
*chaityas*, 37, 137, 139. See also
    *stupas*
compassion, 66
Conditioned Arising, 21–22
cosmology, 2–5
councils: first Buddhist council, 58,
    64, 80; second Buddhist
    council, 35, 58; third Buddhist
    council, 41, 82, 87
cremation of the Buddha, 45–46

Dalai Lama, 73, 76
*dana*, 30, 34, 70
Deer Park, 13, 48, 52
devas, xix–xx, xxii–xxv; in Buddha's
    life story, 7–8; in Buddhist
    cosmology, 3–4
*Dhammacakkapavattana Sutta*, 106.
    See also *Dharmacakrapravartana
    Sutra*
*Dhammapada*, 112–116
*dharmacakra mudra*, 49, 52, 63, photo
    3
*Dharmacakrapravartana Sutra*, 15.
    See also *Dhammacakkapavattana
    Sutta*
*Dharma Yatra. See* Ashoka,
    pilgrimage of

*Diamond Sutra*, 137–140
*Digha Nikaya*, xxxi, 79, 95, 124
Dipankara, 2
dukkha, Buddha's early encounter
    with, 8, 10–12, 17, 99

Eightfold Path, 18–19, 106–108
emptiness, 65, 88–89, 135–140
ethics, 18, 39

Faxian, 51, 54, 83–84
female figures, 63
female monks, 79–80, 119–123
Fire Sermon, 111
first sermon, 13–15. See also
    *Dhammacakkapavattana Sutt*;
    *Dharmacakrapravartana Sutra*
footprint of the Buddha, 48,
    photo 6
Foucher, Alfred, 48
Four Noble Truths, 16–18,
    106–110

Gandhara, 49, 83, 92
Geertz, Clifford, 1
Great *Stupa*, 52–53, 157, photo 6,
    photo 8

*Heart Sutra*, 135–137
Hinduism, xix–xx

iconography, 62
images, 47–48, 54
Impermanence, 21, 95
Indra, xxiv–xxv

Jainism, xx, xxxii, 29
Jains, xxxi–xxxii
*Jatakas*, 4–5, 64; in art, 48, 52–53
*jati. See* caste

*karma*, 20–21
Kassapa. *See* Maha Kashyapa
*Katha Upanishad*, xxx
*kayas*, 55, 59
Krishna, 71
Kshatriyas, xxvi; Buddha as, 5, 14
Kushana dynasty, 70
Kushinagara, 44, 50

*lakshanas*, 49
*Light of Asia*, 74
Lotus Sutra, 140–143
Lumbini, 4–5, 40, 48, 50–51

Madhyamaka, 81
Mahabodhi Temple, 51, photo 4
Mahakashyapa (Maha Kassapa),
    24–25, 84–85
Mahamaya 5–6, 53
Maha Moggallana 84, 85–87
*Mahaparinibbanna Sutta*, 50, 79, 124.
    See also *Mahaparinirvana Sutra*
*mahaparinirvana*, photo 7
*Mahaparinirvana Sutra*, 22, 46. See
    also *Mahaparinibbanna Sutta*
Mahaprajapati Gautami
    (Mahapajapati Gotami), 27, 79,
    87, 117–123
Mahasamghikas, 25, 58–59, 67
Mahavira, Vardhamana, xx, xxxii
Mahayana, 25
Mahinda, 41, 87–88
Maitreya, 2, 62, 79, photo 1
*Majjhima Nikaya*, 10–11, 13
Manjushri, 62
*mantras*, 72
Mara, 4, 12, 103–106, photo 5
Mathura, 49
Mauryan dynasty, 37, 81
*maya*, as illusion, xxiv, xxix

Maya. *See* Mahamaya
meditation, xx, 18, 23, 26, 35, 43,
    45, 72; Ajivaka and Jain, xxxi;
    Buddha's early experience with,
    10–12; images, 50, 53;
    *Upanishads*, xxix; *Vedas*, xxiii;
    Zen, 75–76
middle path, 15, 107
Milinda, 21, 36, 129–132
*Milindapanha*, 129–132
Moggallana. *See* Maha
    Moggallana
monasteries, 26, 33–35
monks: forest, 26, 35; town or
    village, 26, 35
*mudras*, 72

Nagarjuna, 64–66, 81, 88–89,
    93
Nagasena, 21, 36, 129–132
*Nidanakatha*, 7
no self, 2, 129. See also *anatman*;
    *anatta*
nuns. *See* female monks

Olcott, Henry Steele, 74

Padmasambhava, 89–90
Pajapati. See *Maha Prajapati
    Gautami*
palace, Buddha's life in, 6–9, 95
Palas, 70
pantheon, 63, 69
Parable of the Burning House, 66
*paramitas*, 61
*parinirvana*, 44
*paticcasamuppada*, 127. See also
    *pratityasamutpada*
Patiliputra, 41, 82
*patimokkha*, 117–119

*Perfection of Wisdom*, 62–63, 65,
    81–82, 135–137. *See also*
    Prajnaparamita
Pilgrimage, 51–52, 54, 94
Pilgrimage of Ashoka. See Ashoka,
    pilgrimage of
Prajapati, xxiv
*prajna*, 19, 65
Prajnaparamita, 63, 135–137
*Prajnaparamita sutra. See Perfection of
    Wisdom*
Prasenajit, 47
*Pratimoksha*, 34. See also *patimokkha*
*Pratityasamutpada*, 21–22, 89, 127
*Pratyekabuddhas*, 59
*Purusha Shukta*, xxvi

Rahula, 7, 9, 91
rain season retreat, 22
Rajagriha (Rajagaha), 24, 36, 48, 58,
    64, 117
*Record of the Buddhist Kingdoms*, 83
relics, 45–46, 88, 124, 137;
    distribution of, 46
*Rig Veda*, xxii, xxiv, xxvi–xxvii
*rishis*, xxiii
ritual, xxi

sacrifice, Vedic, xxi–xxvii, 111; in
    *Upanishads*, xxviii–xxx
*sadhanas*, 72
*samadhi*. See meditation
Samsara, 19–20
*Samyutta Nikaya*, 111
Sanchi, 4, 48, 50, 52–53, photo 8
*sangha*, 14, 23, 59
Sanskrit, xxi
Sariputta (Shariputra), 84–86,
    91–92, 135–137, 141–145
Sarnath, 13, 48, 50, 52, photo 3

Sarvastivadins, 58–59, 64, 80,
    92
Sazuki, D. T., 76
schisms, 24, 58
Shariputra. *See* Sariputta
*shila. See* ethics
*shramanas*, xx, xxxi, 11–12, 20, 99
*shruti*, xxi
Shuddhodhana, 7
Shudras, xxvi
*shunyata. See* emptiness
*Siddhartha*, xiii, xix, 5, 16, 21, 36,
    50–51, 87, 95, 99, 103, 145,
    148; early life of, 6–8;
    enlightenment of, 10–12. *See
    also* Buddha, names of
Siddhas, 72
Silk Route, 32, 75
*skandhas*, 132, 135
skillful means, 65–66, 140
*soma*, xxiii–xxiv
Sthaviras, 25, 67
*stupas*, 37, 46–49, 51–53, 62, 81, 88,
    137. *See also* Great *Stupa*
Sujata, 12, 52, 103
*Sutra (Pitaka)*, 23, 25, 82

*tanha*, 16
Tantra, 72, 89
*tapas*, xxii–xxiii, xxx
Tara, 63
Tathagata, 15
Theosophical Society, 74
thirty-two auspicious marks. See
    *lakshanas*
Three Refuges, xiv
Tibetan Buddhism, 76–77, 81, 89
trade, xx, 32
*Tripitaka*, 23
Two Truths, 66

Udraka Ramaputra, 10, 13
Upali, 24
*Upanishads*, xv, xx, xxviii–xxxi, 10, 20
*upaya*. See skillful means
urbanization, 30–31

*vac*, xxi
Vaishali (Vesali), 25, 58, 87
Vaishnava, 70–71
Vaishyas, xxvi
Vajra Asana, 51
Vajrayana, 72, 76, 89
*varnas. See* caste
Vasubandhu, 80, 92–93
*Vedas*, xix–xxvii
Vesali. *See* Vaishali
*Vessantara Jataka*, 5
*Vinaya*, 23–25, 32–33, 57, 64, 82, 92

Vishnu, 71
*Visuddhimagga*, 82–83, 127–129, 132–135
Vulture's Peak, 36

Yama, xxvii, xxx
Yashodhara, 7, 9, 91
Yijing, 83
yoga, xxix
Yogacara, 80–81, 93–94

wheel of *dharma*, 14–15, 47, 52, 106
women, status of in Buddhism, 119–123
worlds. *See* cosmology
worship, 49

Xuanzang, 54, 83, 93–94

Zen, 75, 77, 81, 84, 93

## About the Author

JACOB N. KINNARD is Associate Professor of Comparative Religious Thought at Iliff School of Theology. He is the author of *Imaging Wisdom: Seeing and Knowing in the Art of Indian Buddhism* and coeditor of *Constituting Communities: Theravada Traditions in South and Southeast Asia.*

**Greenwood Guides to**
**Historic Events of the Ancient World**

The Peloponnesian War
*Lawrence Tritle*

The Reign of Cleopatra
*Stanley Burstein*

The Decline and Fall of the Roman Empire
*James W. Ermatinger*

The Trojan War
*Carol G. Thomas and Craig Conant*

The Emperor Justinian and the Byzantine Empire
*James Allan Evans*

The Establishment of the Han Empire and Imperial China
*Grant Hardy and Anne Behnke Kinney*